CCNA 2.0 640-507 Routing and Switching Cheat Sheet

by Joe Habraken

201 W. 103rd Street, Indianapolis, Indiana 46290 USA

CCNA 2.0 640-507 Routing and Switching Cheat Sheet

Copyright © 2001 by Que

International Standard Book Number: 0-7897-2293-3

Library of Congress Catalog Card Number: 99-069105

Printed in the United States of America

First Printing: October 2000

02 01   4 3 2

Trademarks

Warning and Disclaimer

Associate Publisher *Greg Wiegand*

Senior Acquisitions Editor *Jenny L. Watson*

Development Editor *Todd Brakke*

Managing Editor *Thomas F. Hayes*

Project Editor *Tonya Simpson*

Copy Editor *Megan Wade*

Indexer *Chris Barrick*

Proofreaders *Jeanne Clark, Katherin Bidwell*

Technical Editor *Clifton L. Stewart*

Team Coordinator *Vicki Harding*

Media Developer *Jay Payne*

Interior Designer *Anne Jones*

Cover Designer *Karen Ruggles*

Production *Ayanna Lacey*

Contents at a Glance

Contents

Chapter 4   The Cisco IOS—Configuration Commands and Passwords

Chapter 5   The Cisco IOS—Configuration Files and IOS Images

Chapter 9   WAN Protocols—HDLC Frame Relay and ATM   169

Chapter 10   WAN Protocols—Configuring PPP and ISDN   193

About the Author

Joe Habraken is a best-selling author whose publications include *The Complete Idiot's Guide to Microsoft Access 2000, Microsoft Office 2000 8 in 1, The Complete Idiot's Guide to Microsoft Windows 2000 Server,* and *Practical Cisco Routers.* Joe has a master's degree from the American University in Washington, D.C., and more than 12 years of experience as an educator, author, and consultant in the information technology field. Joe is a Microsoft Certified Professional and Cisco Certified Network Associate. Joe currently serves as a technical director for ReviewNet Corporation and also is an instructor at the University of New England in Portland, Maine, where he teaches IT certification courses.

Dedication

To my Uncle Wayne and my Aunt Catherine (Cackie) with much love. The times I spent at your house when I was growing up are some of my fondest memories. And I still drink tea!

Acknowledgments

I would like to thank Bill Morter, the network administrator at Globe College, for his help in assembling the equipment that was used to test the information in this book, and Bill Peterson at Nosret Systems in St. Paul, who loaned me a custom-built, high-end Windows server for use on my lab internetwork. And as always, I must thank my incredible wife Kim, who, while pursuing a career of her own, makes sure that I get fed and lovingly tolerates my long hours in the basement "Frankenstein" lab.

And I cannot thank enough the team at Que; creating a book like this takes a real team effort, and this particular book was created by a team of incredibly dedicated professionals. I would like to thank Jenny Watson, my acquisitions editor, who worked very hard to assemble the team who made this book a reality and always made sure the right pieces ended up in the right places. Jenny is a pleasure to work with.

I would also like to thank Todd Brakke, who served as the development editor for this book and who came up with many great ideas for improving its content. He always asked the right questions and wasn't afraid to burn the midnight oil to get the job done.

Also a tip of the hat and a thanks to Clifton Stewart, who as the technical editor for the project did a fantastic job ensuring that everything was correct and suggested a number of additions that made the book even more technically sound. Finally, a great big thanks to our project editor, Tonya Simpson, who ran the last leg of the race and made sure the book made it to press on time—what a great team of professionals. And no acknowledgement can be complete without thanking Jill Hayden at Que, who worked very hard to put the specifications together for the Que *Cheat Sheet* books.

Tell Us What You Think!

As the reader of this book, *you* are our most important critic and commentator. We value your opinion and want to know what we're doing right, what we could do better, what areas you'd like to see us publish in, and any other words of wisdom you're willing to pass our way.

As an Associate Publisher for Que, I welcome your comments. You can fax, email, or write me directly to let me know what you did or didn't like about this book—as well as what we can do to make our books stronger.

Please note that I cannot help you with technical problems related to the topic of this book, and that due to the high volume of mail I receive, I might not be able to reply to every message.

When you write, please be sure to include this book's title and author as well as your name and phone or fax number. I will carefully review your comments and share them with the author and editors who worked on the book.

Fax: 317-581-4666

Email: opsys@mcp.com

Mail: Greg Wiegand
            Que
            201 West 103rd Street
            Indianapolis, IN 46290 USA

The Cisco Certified Network Associate exam (640-507) is the entry-level exam for candidates pursuing the Cisco Certified Internetwork Engineer career track. And although this exam is characterized as entry level, it requires knowledge of networking and internetworking that surpasses many of the other certifications currently available in the Information Technology arena. Passing the CCNA exam provides you with an excellent addition to your rèsumè and shows prospective employers that you have a good working knowledge of many subject areas related to Cisco routers and internetworking.

This book's goal is to help you pass the CCNA exam. The book is broken down into 12 chapters that map to specific categories of subject matter provided by Cisco (such as "Bridging/Switching," "Network Protocols," "Routing," and so on). Cisco actually provides nine categories of subject matter; however, to provide you with a balanced coverage of the material (and to emphasize subject areas that will be emphasized on the exam), some categories have been spread over two chapters.

Cisco also provides a list of objectives under each subject area category. Objective lists are provided in each chapter and map directly to the Cisco CCNA Objectives. In addition, a complete Cisco Exam Outline and Preparation Guide is in the appendix of this book with the objectives mapped to the chapters in which they are covered.

As you move through the chapters in the book, you are moving through the subject categories as dictated by Cisco. However, some subject areas, such as "Bridging/Switching" and "WAN Protocols," have been moved further into the book to provide you with a better stepping-stone approach to the knowledge base you must acquire to pass the test.

Each chapter also provides a practice examination that enables you to test your knowledge of the material in a particular chapter. A "Cheat Sheet" short list of information follows each exam; it provides a quick summary of the chapter and a study resource for memorizing important information from the chapter. Use the short lists as a way to get ready for the exam in those final minutes before taking your seat at the testing center.

A "comprehensive exam" is also provided on the CD that accompanies the book, which will enable you to put your study materials aside and actually test your knowledge base. The final practice exam simulates the CCNA exam (in its multiple-choice format), and you should probably complete all the objectives in the book before taking this final practice exam.

How This Book Is Different

This book is designed to help you pass the CCNA (640-507) exam. It briefly and concisely covers each objective provided by Cisco for the Cisco Certified Network Associate exam. The book is not meant to be an exhaustive tome on internetworking or a primer book on Cisco routers. We want to summarize all the important information for you and provide you with a roadmap to success for the CCNA exam itself.

The book also assumes that you will log some time on a Cisco router and work with the various IOS commands discussed in the book. Screen captures are provided that show you the router console screen results for a particular command; you can use these screens as a reference as you actually execute the commands on a Cisco router.

How to Use This Book

Read through each chapter to get a complete overview of the subject matter for each CCNA objective. You also should use the short lists to reaffirm this knowledge.

After you feel comfortable with each chapter, use the chapter practice exam to identify areas you still need more time with. Explanations of incorrect and correct answers are provided for each exam question to help you learn the chapter subject matter.

After completing the chapter practice exam, you can return to the chapter to review information you hadn't assimilated the first time through the material. Remember that the short lists also provide a quick summary of the vital information in each chapter.

Before taking the actual CCNA exam, you also should review the exam preparation material provided in "The Student Preparation Guide." Cisco takes its certifications very seriously, and this appendix provides some tips and hints on study habits and taking exams.

Working in the internetworking field and working with Cisco routers and switches is very exciting and rewarding. Good luck with your CCNA exam!

The OSI Reference Model

Cisco has divided its CCNA exam objectives into nine categories. The second category of subject matter is the "OSI Reference Model and Layered Communication." This chapter covers four of the required objectives found in the "OSI Reference Model and Layered Communication" category (see the following list):

- Layer definitions
- Layer functions
- Encapsulation/de-encapsulation
- Model benefits

Layer Definitions

In the late 1970s, the International Standards Organization (ISO) began to develop a conceptual model for networking called the *Open Systems Interconnection Reference Model.* It is commonly known as OSI. In 1984, the model became the international standard for network communications, providing a conceptual framework that describes network communication as a series of seven layers; each layer is responsible for a different part of the overall process of moving data.

Although this framework of a layered stack is conceptual, it is used by engineers, technical experts, and system administrators to discuss and understand actual protocol stacks. TCP/IP and IPX/SPX are two real-world network protocol stacks; the different protocols that make up these protocol suites can then be discussed in light of the theoretical layers found in the OSI model. Table 1.1 lists the layers of the OSI model and briefly describes their role in the process of moving data between computers on a network.

Table 1.1 The OSI Layers

Layer Number	Layer	Function
7	Application	Provides the interface and services that support user applications and provides general access to the network.
6	Presentation	The translator of the OSI model; responsible for the conversion of data into a generic format and the coding of data using various encryption methods.

Table 1.1 continued

Layer Number	Layer	Function
5	Session	Establishes and maintains the communication link between communicating computers (sending and receiving).
4	Transport	Responsible for end-to-end data transmission, flow control, error checking, and recovery.
3	Network	Provides the logical addressing system used to route data from one node to another.
2	Data Link	Responsible for the framing of data packets and the data movement across the physical link between two nodes.
1	Physical	Manages the process of sending and receiving bits over the physical network media (the wire and other physical devices).

A good way to remember the network layers from bottom to top is the following mnemonic: Please Do Not Throw Sausage Pizza Away. Make sure you memorize and understand the OSI model and know the layer numbers from bottom up. Sometimes layers are referred to by number, such as "a layer 3 process." You must know that the Network layer is layer 3.

Now that you've had a general introduction to the OSI model, let's take a look at each layer.

Layer Functions

The Cisco CCNA 2.0 exam emphasizes the theoretical aspects of the OSI model, more than you might imagine. It is important that you can quickly recall the function of each layer and how that layer relates to real-world protocols, such as those found in the TCP/IP stack and the Novell IPX/SPX stack. A summary of each layer's function follows with examples of actual protocols that operate at the particular layer discussed.

Application Layer

The Application layer provides the tools the user actually sees (but handles processes the user does not see). Because it is at the top of the OSI model, it does not provide services to layers above it, but it does provide network services related to user applications, such as message handling, file transfer, and database queries. It also synchronizes applications between the client and server and ensures that the resources are available for error recovery and to provide data integrity.

Examples of information exchange services handled by the Application layer include the World Wide Web, email services (such as the Simple Mail Transfer Protocol found in TCP/IP), and special client/server database applications.

An example of Application layer processes is when a user working in a particular application, such as a spreadsheet program like Excel, decides to save a worksheet file to his home directory on the network file server. The Application layer provides the services that enable the file to be moved from the client machine to the network volume. This transaction is transparent to the user.

Presentation Layer

The Presentation layer can be considered the translator of the OSI model. This layer takes the data from the Application layer and converts it to a format that can be read by the Application layer of the receiving computer. The Presentation layer is also responsible for data encryption (if required by the application used in the Application layer) and data compression that will reduce the size of the data.

Several Presentation layer standards exist for various data types, such as text, sound, graphics, and video. Table 1.2 supplies some of these standards and their associated data types.

Table 1.2 Presentation Layer Standards

Data Type	Presentation Layer Standard
Text	ASCII, EBCDIC, HTML
Sound	MIDI, MPEG, WAV
Graphics	JPEG, GIF, TIFF
Video	AVI, QuickTime

Remember that the Presentation layer is the only layer in the OSI stack that can perform data conversion. It basically provides Application layer applications with a choice of data types for transmission over the wire. For example, if an application sends data in binary (pretty much the coin of the realm—recognized by every node), no further action is required by the Presentation layer. The binary data can be read by the receiving computer. However, if the data is sent in another standard, such as EBCDIC (a coding system developed by IBM—Extended Binary Coded Decimal Interchange Code), the Presentation layer might need to convert this to ASCII for the benefit of the receiving computer.

Session Layer

The Session layer is responsible for setting up the communication link or session between the sending and receiving computers. This layer also manages the session that is set up between these nodes.

After the session is set up between the participating nodes, the Session layer is also responsible for placing checkpoints in the data stream. This provides some fault tolerance to the communication session. For example, if the session fails and communication is lost between the nodes, after the session is re-established, only the data after the most recently received checkpoint will need to be resent. This therefore negates the need to tie up the network by resending all the packets involved in the session.

The Session layer offers three different modes of communication: simplex, half-duplex, and full-duplex. *Simplex* transmits data in only one direction (such as your thermostat connecting to your furnace). *Half-duplex* enables communication in two directions but enables the transmission of data in only one direction at a time. *Full-duplex* enables communication in both directions at the same time. Several Session layer protocols exist, such as NetBIOS (highly prevalent in Microsoft networking) and SQL.

Transport Layer

The Transport layer is responsible for the flow control of data between the communicating nodes; data must be delivered error free and also in the proper sequence. The Transport layer is also responsible for sizing the packets so that they are in a size required by the lower layers of the protocol stack. This segmenting is dictated by the network architecture, such as Ethernet, Token-Ring, or FDDI.

The Transport layer provides two different methods of data delivery: connection-oriented and connectionless. *Connection-oriented* protocols at the Transport layer use a system of acknowledgements to ensure data delivery. This is considered a reliable connection. On the other hand, *connectionless* protocols at the Transport layer do not use acknowledgements and are considered unreliable because no mechanism exists to ensure that the data was received. (Connectionless protocols require less system overhead, however, and are used for the movement of data.)

Protocols such as the Transport Control Protocol, User Datagram Protocol (both in the TCP/IP stack), and the Sequence Packet Exchange Protocol (a Novell stack protocol) reside at the Transport layer. More about the Transport layer and flow control and connection issues can be found in Chapter 2, in Objective 7, "Flow Control and Windowing."

Network Layer

The Network layer addresses packets for delivery and is also responsible for their routing. Route determination takes place at this layer, as does the actual switching of packets on to that route. Routers operate at the Network layer and use Layer 3 routing protocols to determine the path for data packets.

Routing protocols such as RIP and IGRP reside at the Network layer, as does the Internet Protocol (all part of the TCP/IP stack). More in-depth coverage of the processes that take place at the Network layer and their relation to routing is covered in Chapter 2, in the section "Network Layer Functions and Internetworking."

Data Link Layer

When the packets reach the Data Link layer, they are placed in data frames defined by the network architecture embraced by your network (such as Ethernet, Token Ring, and so on). The Data Link layer is responsible for data movement across the actual physical link to the receiving node; therefore, it uniquely identifies each computer on the network by the hardware address burned into the network interface card. (Router LAN interfaces are also uniquely identified by these MAC hardware addresses.)

Header information is added to each frame containing the sending address and the destination address. The Data Link layer is also responsible for ensuring that the frames sent over the physical link are received error-free. So, protocols operating at this layer will add a *cyclical redundancy check* (CRC) as a trailer on each frame. The CRC check is basically a mathematical calculation that takes place on the sending computer and then on the receiving computer. If the two CRCs match up, the frame was received in total and its integrity was maintained during transfer.

The Data Link layer is further divided by the IEEE (Institute for Electrical and Electronic Engineers). The IEEE 802 specifications divide the Data Link layer into two sublayers: Logical Link Control (LLC) and Media Access Control (MAC). Issues and specifications related to the Logical Link Control sublayer and the Media Access Control sublayer are covered in Chapter 2, in Objective 8, "IEEE Standards."

Physical Layer

The Physical layer defines the electrical, mechanical, and functional specifications for activating and deactivating the physical link between nodes on the network. So, hubs, repeaters, and the physical wiring of your network reside at the Physical layer.

At the Physical layer, the frames passed down from the Data Link layer are converted into a single bitstream that can then be sent out onto the network media. The Physical layer also defines the actual physical aspects of how the cabling is hooked to the computer's NIC. On a computer that is receiving data, the Physical layer receives the bitstream (information consisting of 1s and 0s).

Encapsulation/De-encapsulation

Now that we've taken a look at the role of each layer in the OSI model, let's take a look at how data moves down through the OSI layers on a sending computer and then how that data, when received by the destination computer, moves up the OSI stack on the receiving computer. The process of data moving from the Application layer to the Physical layer on the sending computer is called *encapsulation*. In addition, the process of data moving up from the Physical layer to the Application layer on the receiving computer is called *de-encapsulation*.

Moving Down the OSI Stack

Cisco expects you to know the five conversion steps of data encapsulation, meaning the transformation that the data undergoes as it moves down the OSI stack. However, you also should be aware of the fact that the data undergoes the exact opposite set of transformations as it moves up the OSI stack on the receiving computer (and undergoes de-encapsulation).

As the data moves down through the OSI layers and the encapsulation process takes place, the original file or information created by the user on the sender computer is transitioned through five different forms: data, segments, packets, frames, and bits:

1. The information generated by the user at the Application layer is converted to *data* and then converted to a format determined by the Presentation layer.

2. After the data has moved down through the Session layer where the session between the sending and receiving computers has been established and synchronized, the data will be converted to *segments* at the Transport layer.

3. These segments are passed on to the Network layer where they are converted to *packets* (also called *datagrams*).

4. Packets move down to the Data Link layer where they are converted to *frames* and then passed down to the Physical layer.

5. At the Physical layer, frames are converted to *bits* and clocking information is added. The bitstream is then transmitted over the network medium.

The following figure shows the data encapsulation conversions as the data moves down through the OSI stack. The opposite takes place as the data moves up the OSI stack on the receiving machine.

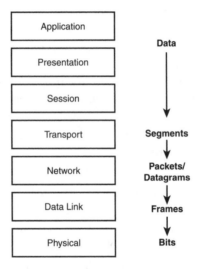

Be sure you remember the five steps of data encapsulation described in this section for the CCNA exam: data (at the Application, Presentation, and Session layers) to segments (at the Transport layer) to packets (at the Network layer) to frames (at the Data Link layer) to bits.

Peer-to-Peer Communication

While data moves down through the protocol stack on the sender's computer (and undergoes the five encapsulation steps) and eventually out onto the wire and then up the protocol stack on the receiving computer (during de-encapsulation), communication does take place between complementary layers on each node. For example, virtual communication occurs between two computers sending and receiving data at the Session layer. This makes sense because this is the layer that controls the communication between the two computers over the network media.

This communication between complementary layers on the sending and receiving computer is called *peer-to-peer communication.* This communication is actually an exchange of information between the protocols operating at a particular layer. This information is called *protocol data units.* The protocol data units exchanged between the Transport layer of the sending and receiving computers will be different from the protocol data units used by another layer, such as the Network layer.

Remember that peer-to-peer communication between layers is not direct communication between layers in the stack. It is the process of peer layers on a receiving computer dealing with data that has been encapsulated at their complementary layer on the sending computer as the data moves back up the OSI stack to the application that will provide the data to the receiving user (such as an FTP client package on the receiving computer). Make sure you understand the concept of peer-to-peer communication for the CCNA exam.

OBJECTIVE 4

Model Benefits

Many reasons exist why a worldwide model was developed for conceptualizing the process of network communication and data transfer. First of all, it divides a complex set of processes into a logical grouping of layers at which certain events take place. This makes it easier to discuss the details of protocol specifications (the OSI model development also probably provided a lot of free lunches for people who sat on the ISO's steering committee when the model was under development). Because the CCNA test is Cisco's test, you should memorize the "Cisco" reasons for having a layered model:

- Complex networking processes are divided into discrete subsets, making it easier for discussion (including teaching and learning).
- It standardizes interfaces between the layers enabling programmers to develop protocols that supply the functionality for a particular layer. This enables "modular" programming.
- Upgrades or enhancements made to one layer are isolated from other layers in the stack.
- It explains the general functions of a layer rather than the specifics.
- It enables specialization (at a particular layer), which enables accelerated evolution of the industry.
- It makes troubleshooting easier.

Another good reason to learn and understand the model (other than passing the CCNA test) is that it is truly used as the conceptual model for all discussions of networking. You will find that no matter what area of networking you specialize in, the OSI model concepts are important to understanding real-world networking and internetworking.

TAKE THE TEST

This Practice Test provides you with questions related to the four CCNA objectives related to the OSI Reference Model and Layered Communication category, which was covered in this chapter. Note that all questions are structured the same as the questions you will find on the actual exam.

1. What are the five steps for data encapsulation?

    A. Bits, Frames, Packets, Segments, Data

    B. Data, Bits, Segments, Frames, Packets

    C. Data, Segments, Packets, Frames, Bits

    D. MIDI, WAV, AVI, ASCII

Answers A and B are incorrect because the sequences are not in the correct order. **Answer C is the correct answer; the encapsulation sequence is data, segments, packets, frames, bits.** Answer D is incorrect; it is a list of coding formats embraced by the Presentation layer.

2. What processes are controlled by the Presentation layer (select all that apply)?

    A. Establish the link between sending and receiving node

    B. Data conversion

    C. Data encryption

    D. Reliable transport of packets

Answer A is incorrect; establishing a link is the responsibility of the Session layer. **The correct answers are B and C. The Presentation layer is responsible for data conversion and encryption.** Answer D is incorrect; reliable transport of packets is a Transport layer function.

3. What layer provides data conversion, such as EBCDIC to ASCII?

A. Application

B. Presentation

C. Data Link

D. Physical

Answer A is incorrect; the Application layer is responsible for program-to-program communication. **Answer B is the correct answer; the Presentation layer is responsible for data conversion.** Answer C is incorrect; the Data Link layer is responsible for the framing and passing of data from one node to another. Answer D is incorrect; the Physical layer places the data onto the network media and takes it off on the receiving computer.

4. What layer establishes communication between nodes across the network?

A. Application

B. Presentation

C. Data Link

D. Session

Answer A is incorrect; the Application layer is responsible for program-to-program communication. Answer B is incorrect; the Presentation layer handles data conversion and encryption. Answer C is incorrect; the Data Link layer handles framing and node-to-node transport. **Answer D is the correct answer; the Session layer establishes the communication session between two nodes on the network.**

5. Select three reasons for the need for a layered network conceptual model.

A. Standardizes interfaces between the layers, enabling programmers to develop protocols that supply the functionality for a particular layer. This enables "modular" programming.

B. Programmers can develop multi-layer protocols that span multiple layers.

C. Upgrades or enhancements made to one layer are isolated from other layers in the stack.

D. It explains the general functions of a layer rather than the specifics.

The correct answers are A, C, and D. The OSI model standardizes interfaces, enabling modular programming; enables upgrades in one layer to be isolated from the other layers; and explains the function of each layer in general terms. Answer B is incorrect; the layered model negates the need for programmers to create protocols that span more than one layer of the OSI model.

6. The Presentation layer provides which data standards (select all that apply)?

   A. JPEG

   B. SQL

   C. MIDI

   D. ASCII

The correct answers are A, C, and D; JPEG, MIDI, and ASCII are all Presentation layer data standards. Answer B is incorrect; SQL is a standard for the Session layer.

7. Which layer of the OSI model handles information exchange services and provides network services for file transfers and message handling?

   A. Application

   B. Presentation

   C. Data Link

   D. Session

Answer A is correct; the Application layer handles information exchange and provides network services for user applications. Answer B is incorrect; the Presentation layer handles data conversion and encryption. Answer C is incorrect; the Data Link layer handles framing and node-to-node transport. Answer D is incorrect; the Session layer establishes and maintains the communications channels between peers.

8. The Data Link layer converts packets to

   A. Data

   B. Bits

   C. Frames

   D. Datagrams

Answer A is incorrect; data is found at the Application, Presentation, and Session layers. Answer B is incorrect; bits are found at the Physical layer. **Answer C is correct; the Data Link layer wraps data from the upper layers in frames.** Answer D is incorrect; datagrams and packets are found at the Network layer.

9. Which layer defines the network's physical topology?

A. Application

B. Presentation

C. Data Link

D. Physical

Answer A is incorrect; the Application layer handles program-to-program communication. Answer B is incorrect; the Presentation layer handles data conversion and encryption. Answer C is incorrect; the Data Link layer handles framing and node-to-node transport. **Answer D is correct; the Physical layer defines the physical topology of the network.**

10. Which layer is responsible for routing on an internetwork?

A. Application

B. Presentation

C. Data Link

D. Network

Answer A is incorrect; the Application layer handles program-to-program communication. Answer B is incorrect; the Presentation layer handles data conversion and encryption. Answer C is incorrect; the Data Link layer handles framing and node-to-node transport. **Answer D is correct; the Network layer is responsible for routing on an internetwork. This is the layer where routers operate.**

Cheat Sheet

The OSI Model (from the top down):

- Application
- Presentation
- Session
- Transport
- Network
- Data Link
- Physical

The Application layer provides network services related to user applications, such as message handling, file transfer, and database queries.

The Presentation layer is the only layer in the OSI stack that can perform data conversion.

The Session layer is responsible for setting up the communication link or session between the sending and receiving computers.

The Transport layer provides two different methods of data delivery: connection-oriented and connectionless.

The Network layer addresses packets for delivery and is also responsible for their routing.

The Data Link layer is responsible for data movement across the actual physical link to the receiving node and is responsible for ensuring that the frames sent over the physical link are received error-free.

The Physical layer defines the electrical, mechanical, and functional specifications for activating and deactivating the physical link between nodes on the network.

The Five Steps of Data Encapsulation:

OSI Layer(s)	Encapsulation Type
Application, Presentation, Session	Data
Transport	Segments
Network	Packets
Data Link	Frames
Physical	Bits

Continued

Peer-to-peer communication takes place between complementary layers of the OSI model on the sending and receiving computers by the exchange of protocol data units.

Reasons for having a layered conceptual model:

- Divides complex systems into discrete and understandable subsets.
- Standardizes layer interfaces for programmers, encouraging modular engineering.
- Isolates upgrades to a layer from other layers in the stack.
- Explains the general function of each layer.

Layered Communication and Connectivity

Cisco has divided its CCNA exam objectives into nine categories. The first category of subject matter is the OSI Reference Model and Layered Communication. This chapter covers two objectives from this category (see the following list). This chapter also covers an objective from the Network Protocols category and two objectives from the Physical Connectivity category (see the following list).

- Connection-Oriented Models
- Connectionless Models
- Windowing (Flow Control)
- IEEE Standards
- ANSI Standards

Connection-Oriented Models

Chapter 1, "The OSI Reference Model," provided an overview of the layers of the OSI model and data encapsulation—both are "must-knows" for the exam. In this chapter, we concentrate on the Transport, Network, and Data Link layers of the OSI model and look at different connection strategies, flow control methods, and physical connectivity standards.

In this section, we concentrate on connection-oriented processes at the Transport layer. And although network communication services can take place at nearly any layer of the OSI model, we typically think of these events as happening at the Session, Transport, and Network layers. The CCNA exam focuses on Transport layer methods used for peer-to-peer communication between nodes on the network. Two possibilities exist: connection-oriented and connectionless (discussed in the next section). Connection-oriented protocols provide best-effort delivery of data between peer computers. This means that delivery is not guaranteed but that mechanisms such as peer acknowledgements, flow control, windowing, and error checking make this a more reliable mode of communication than a connectionless session (windowing is discussed later in this chapter).

Connection-oriented communication is similar to using the telephone. A direct connection is set up between the sending and receiving computers. However, the connection is not guaranteed (for example, you can get a busy signal when making a phone call, the call can become disconnected, or the phone lines can become overburdened by other calls). Connection-oriented sessions require greater network overhead (because acknowledgements are sent between peer computers) and are used by upper-layer protocols (such as protocols residing at the Application layer) that need a reliable connection. This use of a connection-oriented session is hard-wired into the application by the application developer.

A good example of a connection-oriented protocol is the TCP/IP Transport layer protocol called TCP (Transport Control Protocol). A comparable protocol in the NetWare IPX/SPX stack is the SPX (Sequenced Packet Exchange) protocol.

Connection-oriented protocols establish a communication session between peer computers. For example, TCP sets up a session using a three-way handshake:

- The sending host sends out a synchronization segment with the synchronization flag set to on to initiate the session.

- The receiving host acknowledges the request from the sending host by sending back a segment with the synchronization flag set to on, a sequence number to indicate the starting byte sequence number that can be sent, and a byte sequence number of the next segment it expects to receive.

- The requesting host sends back a segment with the acknowledged sequence number and acknowledgement number.

Connection-oriented protocols use this system of acknowledgements to determine whether segments need to be resent (if no acknowledgement is received from the receiving peer computer, segments are resent). Connection-oriented protocols are, in effect, setting up a virtual circuit (like a telephone call) between the sending and receiving peers. Remember that connection-oriented protocols are characterized by their error recovery capabilities and the fact that they use a pre-established path through the network (the virtual circuit).

6

Connectionless Models

Connectionless protocols operate more like the regular mail system. They provide appropriate addressing for the packets that must be sent, and then the packets are sent off much like a letter dropped in the mailbox. It is assumed that the addressing on the packet will get it to its final destination, but no acknowledgement is required from the computer that is the intended destination.

Connectionless services do not use a predetermined path through the network, nor do they have flow control or other mechanisms for ensuring the dedication of network resources. Connectionless services must completely address their packets because packets might not take the same path through the network. This means that a dynamic path is selected for the data on a packet-by-packet basis. User Datagram Protocol (UDP), a Transport layer protocol in the TCP/IP stack, is a good example of a connectionless, best effort, delivery protocol. The IP protocol at the Network layer is another example of a connectionless protocol.

Flow Control and Windowing

As already mentioned in the section "Connection-Oriented Models," connection-oriented network services use flow control to help guarantee delivery from sending to receiving computers. The purpose of flow control is to ensure that the segments are sent in such a way that the receiving computer is not overwhelmed by the amount of data sent. Flow control mechanisms help diminish congestion on the network. Although the Cisco CCNA 2.0 preparation guidelines specify windowing as an objective, three basic methods are actually used for flow control: buffering, congestion avoidance (through the use of source-quench messaging), and windowing. You should understand all three of these flow control methods for the exam.

Buffering is a network device (such as a computer or router) that allocates memory that is used to hold data waiting to be processed. This means that occasional data bursts can be held in the buffer until they can be processed. Large amounts of data can cause buffer overflow, meaning data will discarded.

Congestion avoidance occurs when a device receives data at a rate that can overflow the buffer memory. Then, the device sends a source-quench message to the sending computer requesting that it reduce the current rate of data transmission. Source-quench messages also can be sent to the sending computer to tell it to stop sending data completely. The receiving device then must send a "start" message to the sending computer when it is ready to receive data again.

Windowing requires that the sending and receiving computers agree on a window size that defines the number of packets that will be sent in each burst of data. The sending computer sends a predetermined number of packets (such as five packets). When the receiving computer receives the five packets, it sends an acknowledgement. The sending computer then sends the next five packets. If the current window size (the five packets) proves to be too much for the receiving computer and its buffer overflows, it does not send an acknowledgement to the sending computer. The sending computer then resends the data using a smaller window size.

IEEE Standards

When you work with internetworking and the movement of data across routed networks, you are actually working with two different addressing systems. *MAC* addresses are supplied by the Data Link layer, and *logical* addresses are supplied by the Network layer. Before discussing these two different addressing systems, both of which play a role in routing data, we'll take a look at the IEEE specifications and their relationship to the Data Link layer.

Remember from Chapter 1 that the Data Link layer is divided into two sublayers: the Media Access Control layer and the Logical Link Control layer. The Media Access Control (MAC) sublayer determines how computers communicate on the network and how and when a computer can actually access the network media and send data.

The Logical Link Control (LLC) sublayer establishes and maintains the link between the sending and receiving computers as data moves across the network's physical media. The LLC sublayer also provides Service Access Points (SAPs), which are reference points that other computers sending information can refer to and use to communicate with the upper layers of the OSI stack on a particular receiving node.

These sublayers were added to the OSI model by the IEEE (Institute for Electrical and Electronic Engineers), and the 802 specifications define the various frame types and media access strategies found at the Data Link layer.

A list of the IEEE specifications for the Data Link layer follows:

- 802.1 Internetworking
- 802.2 Logical Link Control
- 802.3 Ethernet(CSMA/CD) LAN
- 802.4 Token Bus LAN
- 802.5 Token-Ring LAN
- 802.6 Metropolitan Area Network

- 802.7 Broadband Technical Advisory Group
- 802.8 Fiber Optic Technical Advisory Group
- 802.9 Integrated Voice and Data Networks
- 802.10 Network Security
- 802.11 Wireless Networks
- 802.12 Demand Priority LAN

Although these specifications seem a little cryptic, an example of how they are actually applied can be related in terms of the Ethernet frame. The 802.3 specification defines the size and components of an Ethernet frame (including things such as the size of the header, the amount of data in the frame, and so on). The IEEE then determined that the 802.3 frame should be modified to include logical link control information. This is defined by 802.2 of the IEEE model. All the 802 specifications relate to different media access strategies, which results in different frame types and data communication standards.

For the exam, remember that 802.3 is the specification for the Ethernet frame, that 802.5 is the specification for the Token-Ring frame, and that both of these specifications refer to processes that take place at the MAC sublayer. Also keep in mind that 802.2 actually defines the Logical Link Control sublayer of the Data Link layer.

Now that we've sorted out some of the IEEE specifications, we can look at how Data Link addressing (as defined by the MAC sublayer) is used by devices on the network to send and receive data.

Data Link Addressing

Data Link addresses, or MAC addresses, are 48-bit addresses that are burned into the ROM of a network interface card (NIC) or a router LAN interface. (They are also referred to as the burned in addresses.) These addresses are expressed as 12 hexadecimal digits, with the first 6 digits specifying the manufacturer of the device and the remaining 6 digits unique to the host device. The MAC address of a NIC that is used on a Windows 98 computer attached to a network appears in the following figure.

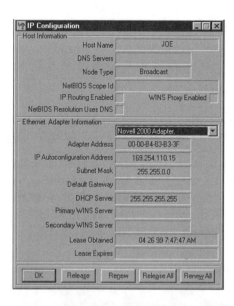

Data Link addresses are referred to as MAC addresses because it is the MAC sublayer of the Data Link layer that interfaces with the network media. MAC addresses can be considered a flat addressing system that uniquely identifies nodes (such as NetBIOS names). Mac addresses can be used to move data locally but are not used to move data over an internetwork (which is the purpose of Network layer addressing such as IP addresses, discussed in the next section).

Remember that the Data Link layer enables the upper layers of the OSI model to basically ignore the type of media used at the Physical layer, and this layer can also supply optional flow control and error notification. Most importantly, the Data Link layer defines the frame type used to encapsulate packets at this layer. WAN protocols, such as HDLC (high-level data link control protocol) and Frame Relay, also operate at the Data Link layer.

When computers ready themselves to send data on a local network, they use some method of determining the MAC address of the receiving node (typically broadcast messages). After the MAC address of the receiving computer is determined, this information can be placed in the frame header. However, MAC addressing does not supply a hierarchical addressing system that enables the routing of data across the internetwork.

Network Layer Addressing

Network addresses are logical addresses used by routers to route packets between local networks or subnets on the internetwork. As you already know from Chapter 1, the Network layer of the OSI model is involved in the path determination for the movement of packets across the internetwork. In addition, the Network layer is where routing protocols, such as the Routing Information Protocol (RIP), operate. Routers function at the Network layer.

Network addresses are hierarchical; they supply both network and node information in one address. Routers use the network portion of the address to determine the best route to a remote computer that is being sent data from a computer that resides on a different network.

An example of a Network layer protocol that supplies a logical addressing scheme is IP (Internet protocol, part of the TCP/IP stack). An IP address, such as 10.1.1.1, can be broken down into a network ID, 10.0.0.0, and a host ID, 0.1.1.1. (An IP address is of no use without the accompanying subnet mask; IP addressing is discussed in Chapter 6.)

MAC Addresses Versus Logical Addresses

You should remember that MAC addresses are unique Data Link layer addresses assigned to devices on the network. MAC addresses are similar to Social Security numbers. They uniquely identify an entity, a computer on the network (just like your Social Security number uniquely identifies you), but they do not provide any information about in which network or location the particular computer resides (just like your Social Security number does not provide information about where you reside).

Logical addresses, such as IP and IPX addresses, provide location information; they tell you where the particular node is on the internetwork. This enables a router to use the logical address to get the packets to the correct local network or subnet.

Network Layer Functions and Internetworking

The Network layer is where path determination across the internetwork is determined for packets. Routers use routing protocols to determine the network map they use for determining the best path for packets and then switch the packets to the appropriate router interface to move the packets onward in their journey to their final destination.

Routers enable you to divide a large network into logical subnets; this keeps network traffic local on each subnet, allowing you to take better advantage of the bandwidth available. It's then the job of the router to move data packets between these subnets when necessary. Routers can also serve as the connective device between your network and other networks to which you might be attached. (All your subnets are viewed by other enterprise networks as a single network even though you've divided them into logical parts, called *subnets*.) The best example of many different networks connected for communication purposes is the Internet.

When a computer on a particular network subnet prepares to send packets to a particular destination computer, the computer uses broadcast messages to determine the hardware address of the destination machine. If the destination machine is on the same local subnet, the destination computer responds with its hardware address, and the sending computer then sends the packets to that particular address.

However, when the destination computer is on a different subnet, the local router becomes involved in the process. The router actually responds to the sending computer's request for a hardware address and supplies the hardware address of its (the router's) LAN interface that is connected to that local subnet. So, the router LAN interface's hardware address is actually incorporated into the frame header of the data.

The sending computer then sends the data to the router. The router examines the logical Network layer address of the packets, and then uses its routing table to determine the best path across the internetwork for the packets. This routing table supplies information on all the router's interfaces (LAN and WAN) and the networks that can be reached through a particular interface.

Using the routing table, the router switches the packets to the appropriate interface, and the packets move on to the next step in their journey. This can be a second router or the final destination subnet. If the packets are only moved to the next hop in their journey and sent to the next router on the internetwork map, that router will determine the best path for the packets using its routing table and then switch the packets to the appropriate interface.

When the packets finally reach the router that services the destination subnet, the router determines the MAC hardware address of the destination computer and places this information in the frame header. Then, when the router places the packets on the destination subnet through the appropriate router interface (determined using the routing table), the packets are accepted by the destination computer, which sees its MAC address on the packet's frame header.

For you to fully understand how routing takes place, you will need to understand how routing tables are built and how routing protocols determine the best path for packets as they are moved on the internetwork. You also must understand how logical addressing systems supply subnetwork or subnet information and node information in one logical address. Chapters 6, "Network Protocols—TCP/IP," and 7, "Network Protocols—IPX/SPX," discuss IP and IPX addressing, respectively. Chapter 8, "Internetwork Routing," discusses routing protocols.

9

ANSI Standards

The American National Standards Institute (ANSI) is an organization of American industry and business groups dedicated to the development of trade and communication standards. ANSI is the American member of the ISO. Although the CCNA exam preparation guide lists ANSI standards as objectives, it is only important that you know who ANSI is and how they have been involved in the standardization of network communications in the United States.

ANSI has developed standards for networking (as already mentioned) and for other areas in the computing arena, including programming and devices. (The SCSI device is a good example of a device that was developed using ANSI standards.) ANSI working groups assign specification numbers to developing technologies just as the IEEE standards are used to provide consistency in the development of Data Link layer processes.

For example, Asymmetrical Digital Subscriber Line technology (or DSL, as it is commonly referred to—a fairly new, high-speed data transfer method over regular phone lines) has been actively pursued by ANSI and has been assigned the ANSI Standard T1.413. Other technologies, such as the 100BASE-TX and 100BASE-FX media standards used in Fast Ethernet, were actually both adopted from physical media standards first developed by ANSI. ANSI also worked on physical media standards for the Fiber Distributed Data Interface (FDDI), which was assigned the ANSI standard X3T9.5.

TAKE THE TEST

This Practice Test provides you with questions related to two of the CCNA objectives from the OSI Reference Model and Layered Communication category, one objective from the Network Protocols category, and two objectives from the Physical Connectivity category. These practice questions are structured the same as the questions you will find on the exam.

1. Connection-oriented protocols set up a _____ between the sending and receiving computer.

   A. Dynamic route

   B. Virtual circuit

   C. Best effort delivery

   D. Route on a packet to packet basis

Answer A is incorrect; a dynamic route is the strategy used by connectionless protocols. **Answer B is the correct answer; connection-oriented protocols set up a virtual circuit between sending and receiving computers.** Answers C and D are also incorrect; they are attributes of a connectionless protocol.

2. Select various methods of flow control (select all that apply).

   A. Framing

   B. Congestion avoidance

   C. Buffering

   D. Windowing

Answer A is incorrect; framing is the encapsulation of packets at the Data Link layer in network architecture frames. **The correct answers are B, C, and D; congestion avoidance, buffering, and windowing are all flow control methods.**

3. The burned-in address for a network interface card is also known as the

A. IP address

B. NetBIOS name

C. MAC address

D. Hierarchical address

Answer A is incorrect; IP addresses are logical addresses. Answer B is incorrect; the NetBIOS name of a computer is also a logical addressing scheme. **Answer C is correct; the burned-in address or hardware address is defined by the Media Access Control sublayer of the Data Link OSI layer.** Answer D is incorrect; the MAC address is a flat hardware address not a hierarchical address, such as IP addresses.

4. Routers use which type of addressing to route packets on the internetwork (select all that apply)?

A. MAC addresses

B. NetBIOS addresses

C. IP addresses

D. IPX addresses

Answer A is incorrect; MAC addresses are used locally on the network subnets to get packets to destination computers. Answer B is incorrect; NetBIOS names are part of a logical system used by transport protocols, such as NetBEUI, which is not routable. **Answers C and D are correct; routers use logical addressing schemes such as IP addresses or IPX addresses to forward packets on the internetwork.**

5. Which of the listed protocols are connectionless (select all that apply)?

A. IP

B. TCP

C. UDP

D. SPX

Answers A and C are correct; IP and UDP are connectionless protocols. Answer B is incorrect; TCP is a connection-oriented protocol. Answer D is incorrect; SPX is a connection-oriented protocol.

6. What is the responsibility of the Network layer of the OSI model?

    A. Framing of packets

    B. Connection-oriented transport

    C. Routing of packets on the internetwork

    D. Setting up a virtual circuit

Answer A is incorrect; the framing of packets is the responsibility of the Data Link layer. Answer B is incorrect; connection-oriented transport is a Transport layer process. **Answer C is correct; the Network layer is responsible for the routing of packets on the internetwork.** Answer D is incorrect; virtual circuits are used at the Transport layer by connection-oriented protocols.

7. What is the IEEE specification for the Logical Link Control sublayer?

    A. 802.3

    B. 802.5

    C. 802.2

    D. 802.6

Answer A is incorrect; this is the specification for Ethernet. Answer B is incorrect; this is the specification for Token-Ring. **Answer C is correct; 802.2 is the IEEE specification for logical link control.** Answer D is incorrect; this is the specification for Token Bus networks.

8. Which is an example of a protocol that uses acknowledgements to set up a virtual circuit between sending and receiving computers?

    A. IP

    B. TCP

    C. UDP

    D. IPX

Answer A is incorrect; IP is a connectionless protocol that does not use a virtual circuit. **Answer B is correct; TCP is a connection-oriented protocol that uses acknowledgements to set up a session between sending and receiving computers.** Answer C is incorrect; UDP is a connectionless protocol. Answer D is incorrect; IPX is a connectionless protocol.

9. Which layer of the OSI model contains the MAC sublayer that defines the network architectures in the IEEE standards?

A. Application

B. Presentation

C. Data Link

D. Physical

Answer A is incorrect; the Application layer provides network services. Answer B is incorrect; the Presentation layer is the translator layer. **Answer C is correct; the Data Link layer contains the MAC sublayer and provides the frame types for the various network architectures.** Answer D is incorrect; the Physical layer defines the network topology.

10. Which of the following statements are true concerning ANSI (select all that apply)?

A. ANSI develops standards in the United States for data communication technologies.

B. ANSI standards were adopted in the development of Fast Ethernet.

C. ANSI is no longer operating and has been replaced by the IEEE.

D. ANSI does not interface with the ISO.

Answer A is correct; ANSI is involved in standardizing data communication in the United States. Answer B is correct; ANSI originally came up with the standards for the technology that became Fast Ethernet. Answer C is incorrect; ANSI is still a viable entity today and operates in parallel with the IEEE. Answer D is incorrect; ANSI is actually the American member of the International Standards Organization (ISO), which developed the OSI model.

Cheat Sheet

Connection-oriented protocols provide best effort (although not guaranteed) delivery of data between peer computers and use mechanisms such as peer acknowledgements, flow control, windowing, and error checking.

Connection-oriented sessions require greater network overhead.

A good example of a connection-oriented protocol is the TCP/IP Transport layer protocol TCP.

Connectionless services do not use a predetermined path through the network, nor do they have flow control or other mechanisms for ensuring the dedication of network resources.

UDP and IP are both good examples of connectionless, best effort, delivery protocols.

Three basic methods are used for flow control: buffering, congestion avoidance, and windowing.

Buffering is accomplished by holding some data in the receiving computer's memory.

Congestion avoidance is accomplished by using source-quench messages that are sent from the receiving computer to the sending computer to slow down data transfer.

Windowing is the process of the sending and receiving computers agreeing on the number of packets that are sent in each data burst on the wire.

The IEEE specifications for the Data Link layer of the OSI model are as follows:

- 802.1 Internetworking
- 802.2 Logical Link Control
- 802.3 Ethernet(CSMA/CD) LAN
- 802.4 Token Bus LAN
- 802.5 Token-Ring LAN
- 802.6 Metropolitan Area Network
- 802.7 Broadband Technical Advisory Group
- 802.8 Fiber Optic Technical Advisory Group

Continued

- 802.9 Integrated Voice and Data Networks
- 802.10 Network Security
- 802.11 Wireless Networks
- 802.12 Demand Priority LAN

MAC addresses are 48-bit addresses that are burned in to the ROM of a network interface card (NIC) or a router LAN interface.

The Network layer provides the mechanisms for path determination and the routing of packets across an internetwork.

ANSI (American National Standards Institute) is an organization of American industry and business groups dedicated to the development of trade and communication standards. ANSI is the American member of the ISO.

The Cisco IOS—Basic Router Commands

Cisco has divided its CCNA exam objectives into nine categories. Category 9, "Cisco Basics, IOS & Network Basics," lists IOS CLI Router as an objective. This is one of the most important objectives for the exam and requires that you know how to execute a wide range of commands from the router's command-line interface. This objective is covered in this chapter and continues in Chapters 4, "The Cisco IOS—Configuration Commands and Passwords," and 5, "The Cisco IOS—Configuration Files and IOS Images." This chapter also covers one objective, Telnet, from the Network Management Category.

- IOS CLI Router
- Telnet

10

IOS CLI Router—Basic Commands

The Cisco Internetworking Operating System (IOS) is the software that provides the router hardware with the capability to route packets on an internetwork. The IOS (just like any other operating system) provides the command sets and software functionality you use to monitor and configure the router, and it also provides the functionality for the various protocols—both routed and routing—that make internetworking a reality.

Cisco provides a command-line interface (CLI) you can use to interact with the router's IOS and maintain and configure your router. You can access the CLI using a router console or by telnetting to a router using a virtual terminal. When you log in to a router, you are placed in the user EXEC mode (one mode of the EXEC command interpreter), meaning that commands typed at the prompt are executed and a response is provided by the IOS on the console or virtual terminal screen.

The user mode enables you to examine the router's settings and telnet out to other routers on the internetwork (if you have the virtual terminal password for the router to which you want to telnet). The user mode enables you to perform only a limited examination of the router and its configuration.

The EXEC command interpreter also has a second mode—the *privileged* mode. The privileged mode provides a larger set of commands than the user mode, enabling you to view your currently running configuration and the startup configuration for the router. It also enables you to copy configuration files and *IOS images* (actual IOS files) to and from the router using a Trivial File Transfer Protocol (*TFTP*) server (more about TFTP in Chapter 5). More importantly, the privileged mode enables you to enter the configuration mode and change the router's configuration (more about router configuration in Chapter 4 when we discuss using the setup command).

You can log in to a router using a console connection, auxiliary connection (enabling you to dial in to the router using a modem), or virtual terminal connection via telnet (by logging in to the router from another host on the network, such as another router; Telnet is discussed later in the chapter). Login is required for only a particular connection (such as from the console or virtual terminal if a login password has been set).

Log In on the Console

The most straightforward method of connecting to a router is to connect a PC that is running a terminal emulation program to the router using the rollover console cable that came with the router. One of the RJ-45 connectors on the cable is connected to the Console port on the back of the router (see the following figure).

The RJ-45 connector on the other end of the cable is connected to a serial adapter that connects to a serial port on the computer.

After the console is connected to the router and a previously configured router is turned on (routers are usually on all the time; otherwise, they wouldn't be routing packets), you can log in to the router:

1. Press Enter to access the login command-line prompt (see the following figure).

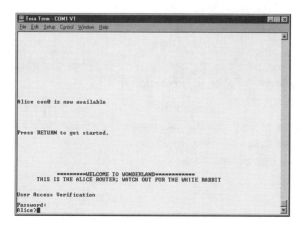

2. Type the console password at the Password prompt.

3. Press Enter to enter the password.

You will be placed in the user EXEC mode on the router.

Entering the Privileged Mode

The privileged mode enables you to access more complete information on the router's configuration and set operating system parameters (you must be in the privileged mode to enter the router's configuration mode). The user mode provides only a subset of the privileged mode commands.

To enter a router's privileged mode, perform the following steps:

1. At the user mode prompt, type **enable** and then press Enter.

2. Type the Enable password at the Password prompt. Keep in mind that if no password was provided, just typing **enable** places the router in privileged mode.

3. Press Enter to enter the password.

As shown in the following figure, the router prompt change from the user mode prompt (the router name followed by the > symbol) to the privileged mode prompt (the router name followed by the # symbol). You can now use the extended command set provided by privileged mode (such as entering the configuration mode).

Remember that the user mode provides only a subset of the router examination commands available in the privileged mode. Also, you must be in the privileged mode to enter the configuration mode.

When you are finished working in the privileged mode, type **disable**, and then press Enter to return to the user mode. If you want to log off the router completely, type **exit** and press Enter.

Router Mode Summary

Before leaving our discussion of router logons and the user and privileged modes, let's summarize the various router modes available. These will show up on the CCNA exam. Although you will mainly work in the user, privileged, and configuration modes, other router modes exist. Table 3.1 provides a summary of these different modes.

Table 3.1 Router Modes

Mode	Use
User	Basic examination of the router status; limited command set; cannot change configuration.
Privileged	Greater examination of router status and configuration; capability to change router status and enter configuration mode.
Configuration	Enables configuration of global router parameters and the entering of specific configuration information for router interfaces and other settings.
RXBOOT	The ROM monitor mode; enables recovery of router functions when the IOS image cannot be found (such as a corrupt IOS image). This mode also can be entered by pressing the Break key on a router console during the first minute of the system bootup (this mode can be used to help recall lost passwords on the router).
Setup	Initiated on a new router or a router that does not have a valid startup configuration. It walks you through the router configuration in the System dialog box.

The IOS Help Facility

No matter which mode you're in, the Cisco IOS can provide you with help. You can view a list of commands available in a particular mode, or you can get context-sensitive help related to a particular command. For a brief description of how the help system works, type **help** or **?** at any prompt, and then press Enter.

For example, let's say that you are in the user mode and want to see a complete list of the commands available. Type **?**, and then press Enter. The commands are listed on the console screen shown in the following figure.

The commands listed by the **?** command will depend on the IOS version with which you are working. You should become familiar with IOS version 11.3 for the CCNA exam. To see your IOS version, use the command show ver.

You can get context-sensitive help for any command by typing the command and following it with a **?**. For example, to see the list of uses for the show command, type **show ?**. You will be provided with help specifically for the show command (see the following figure).

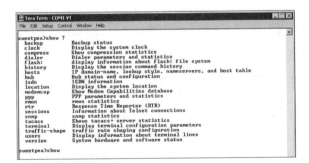

After the help for the specific command is listed, you are returned to the router prompt with the command already entered. All you have to do is enter other necessary parameters (listed in the context-sensitive help) to complete the command. Next, press Enter to enter the command after providing the additional parameters.

You can also get a list of commands that start with a particular letter or abbreviation. Type the letter or abbreviation at the prompt immediately followed by a **?**, and then press Enter. For example, typing **s?** at the user prompt provides a list of the commands show, slip, set, and systat (all the commands that start with the letter s). To get additional help on these commands, type the complete command and follow it with a question mark.

When the information provided by a particular command, such as ?, doesn't fit on one console screen, More appears at the bottom of the displayed information. To move down through the additional information, press Enter to advance one line and press the spacebar to advance one screen. If you don't want to view more information and want to return to the console prompt, press Esc.

Command History and Editing Features

The IOS also provides you with some shortcuts related to entering commands at the EXEC prompt. One method is to abbreviate commands; for example, sh for the command show. A very quick way to enter a previously used command is to use the Command History. The Command History provides you with a list of your most recently used commands (the last 10 commands). To cycle through the commands (most recent to least recent) press the up-arrow key (the down-arrow key moves you in the opposite direction through the list). You can view a list of the commands in the History buffer using the command show history.

You can change the number of commands that are available in the Command History buffer. Use the terminal history size [*number*] command, where the *number* is the number of commands you want to be saved in the Command History. This command must be used at the privileged prompt (see the following figure).

The IOS also provides several editing commands that can be used to edit or modify a command at the EXEC prompt. Table 3.2 summarizes these editing commands.

Table 3.2 IOS Editing Commands

Command Keys	Result
Ctrl+A	Moves the cursor to the beginning of the command line
Ctrl+E	Moves the cursor to the end of the command line
Esc+F	Moves the cursor forward one word on the command line
Esc+B	Moves the cursor back one word on the command line
Backspace	Moves back one character on the command line, deleting the character to the left of the cursor
Ctrl+F	Moves forward one character from the cursor
Ctrl+B	Moves backward one character from the cursor
Command abbreviation followed by Tab	Completes the abbreviated command (sh becomes show)
Ctrl+P	Same as the up arrow, shows most recent command in History
Ctrl+N	Same as down arrow, moves backward through the History

These command-line editing shortcuts are enabled on a router by default. They can be disabled using the command terminal no editing (executed at the privileged prompt). If you find that you can use these editing shortcuts, though, you can enable them by executing the terminal editing command at the privileged prompt.

The show Command

When you work in the EXEC modes (user and privileged), several of the commands you use center around examining the various configuration settings and hardware parameters of the router. It has already been mentioned that user mode provides you with a set of commands you can use to examine the router status and that it is actually a subset of commands available to you in the privileged mode.

One of the most useful EXEC commands is show (this cannot be stressed enough). It can tell you everything from the system clock settings to the contents of the running configuration file. The show command will be looked at in more detail at the end of this section.

Another aspect of examining the router status is viewing your current configurations (both the running configuration and the stored startup configuration) and the IOS image (the IOS image is the binary operating system file running on the router). Before we examine these various configurations and IOS image, it makes sense to understand how and where the router stores these various items. The router actually uses different types of memory to run and store files.

Router Memory Types

Cisco routers actually contain different types of memory components that provide the storage and dynamic caching required. The following list provides information about the various memory components found in a Cisco router.

- **ROM**—Contains the power-on self test and the bootstrap program for the router. The ROM chips also contain either a subset or the complete router IOS (for example, the ROM on the 2505 router contains only a subset of the IOS, whereas the 7000 series contains the full IOS). The fact that the IOS is available on the ROM enables you to recover from major disasters, such as the wiping out of your Flash RAM (discussed in the following paragraphs). The ROM chips on Cisco routers are removable and can be upgraded or replaced.

- **NVRAM (nonvolatile RAM)**—Stores the startup configuration file for the router. NVRAM can be erased, and you can copy the running configuration on the router to NVRAM. The great thing about NVRAM is that it retains the information it holds even if the router is powered down (which is extremely useful considering you won't want to have to reconfigure the router every time the power goes down).

- **Flash RAM**—Flash is a special kind of ROM that you can actually erase and reprogram. It is used to store the Cisco IOS that runs on your router. You also can store alternative versions of the Cisco IOS on the Flash.

- **RAM**—Similar to the dynamic memory you use on your PC, RAM provides the temporary storage of information and holds information such as the current routing table. RAM also holds the currently running router configuration (changes that you make to the configuration are kept in RAM until you save them to NVRAM).

Examining RAM, NVRAM, and Flash RAM

Several items reside in the router's RAM (while the router is powered on), including the router's active IOS, the running configuration, the routing table, and other cache and buffers (such as the History buffer). You can view these items using various permutations of the show command.

For example, to view the router's running configuration, you would use the show running-config command at the privileged prompt (see the following two figures—the results of the command are selectively shown).

This command provides configuration information (such as passwords and the banner for the router) and the current status of the router's interfaces.

Another useful command related to the router's RAM is the show version command. This enables you to view the version of the IOS that is currently running on the router.

RAM also provides the temporary storage area for your routing tables. Routing tables and routing IP and IPX are discussed later in this book. To view the current routing table for a network protocol such as IP, you would use the show ip route command. The following figure shows the results of this command. Routes labeled with a C are directly connected routes, whereas routes labeled with an R were learned by the routing protocol running on the router.

NVRAM supplies the nonvolatile storage area for your startup configuration. The output of the show startup-config command looks much the same as the running-config command displayed in the previous two figures. However, it can be different from that command, and it is also a privileged mode command.

Flash RAM is where the current image of the system IOS resides. If your router has enough Flash RAM, alternative versions of the IOS can also be stored there (other than the IOS image that's loaded when the router is powered on). This is useful in cases where you plan to upgrade the IOS on all your routers at once because the new IOS is immediately available for deployment.

To view the contents of the Flash RAM, use the command show flash. The next figure shows the results of this command.

The Cisco Discovery Protocol

The Cisco IOS contains a proprietary protocol, Cisco Discovery Protocol (CDP), which enables you to access information related to neighboring routers. CDP uses Data Link broadcasts to discover neighboring Cisco routers that are also running CDP (CDP is turned on automatically on routers running IOS 10.3 or later). CDP is platform-independent, so it will accumulate information about neighbor routers no matter which network protocol stack they might be running (such as TCP/IP, IPX/SPX, and so on).

To view the CDP interfaces on the router, use the command show cdp interface (see the following figure). This command provides the CDP information for all enabled interfaces on the router. To view CDP stats on one interface, such as Serial 0, use the show cdp interface s0 command.

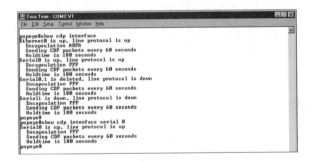

Two pieces of information shown in the results of the show cdp interface command warrant further discussion: the CDP packet send interval and the *CDP holdtime.* Notice that CDP packets are sent by CDP-enabled interfaces every 60 seconds. This means that they are broadcasting information to their CDP neighbors every minute.

The holdtime refers to the amount of time a router should hold the CDP information it has received from a neighboring router. If a router does not receive an update message from a neighbor within 3 minutes (180 seconds), it must discard the old CDP information it holds.

If the show cdp interface command provides no results or does not provide information for a particular interface, CDP is not enabled. CDP can be disabled globally or on an interface-by-interface basis. To disable CDP globally, enter the configuration mode and then type **no cdp run**. This shuts it off on all interfaces. For a particular interface, enter the configuration mode and specify the interface you want to disable; then use the command **no cdp enable**. The global command for turning on CDP is **cdp run**.

After you have viewed the status of CDP on your various interfaces, you can use CDP to take a look at platform and protocol information on a neighboring router or routers. At the user or privileged prompt, type **show cdp neighbors**, and then press Enter (see the next figure).

Table 3.3 describes the information show in the figure.

Table 3.3 The show Command in the User Mode

Parameter	Means	Information from the Figure
Device ID	The neighbor or neighbors' hostname(s)	sweetpea
Local Interface	The interface on the local router that provides the connection to the neighbor	Ser 0
Capacity	Whether the router is configured to serve multiple functions such as routing (R), bridging (B), and switching (S)	R T (this router is configured to route and bridge)
Platform	The type of Cisco router	2516 (the neighbor is a 2516 router)
Port ID	The interface used on the neighbor to connect to your local router	Serial 0

Obviously, if you have a router connected to many different neighbors via its various interface ports, the number of neighbors shown using the show cdp neighbor command would provide information on several routers.

If you want to see more details concerning your CDP neighbors, you can use the show cdp neighbor detail command, which you can enter at the user or privileged prompt. This command provides the IP address of the neighbor's interface and the version of the IOS the neighbor is running.

To view CDP statistics related to one CDP neighbor, use the show cdp entry [router name] command, in which you specify the router name of the neighbor.

More About show

As you've already seen in the previous sections, one of the most useful commands on the router is the show command. You can use this command to view the status of all the interfaces on the router and the network protocols currently being routed. The more you know about how to use show in different instances, the better you will do on the CCNA exam. Table 3.4 provides a summary of some of the more useful show commands.

Table 3.4 Router Examination Commands

Command	Results
show running-config	Privileged command that shows the router configuration currently running in RAM.
show startup-config	Privileged command that shows the router configuration stored in the router's NVRAM. It's loaded by the router when the router is rebooted.
show CDP neighbor	Shows the routers that are directly connected to your router by LAN or serial connections.
show clock	Shows the time and date settings for the router.
show flash	Shows the IOS file or files contained in the router's Flash RAM and the amount of total Flash RAM and used Flash RAM.
show history	Shows a list of your last 10 commands.

Table 3.4 continued

Command	Results
show hub	Shows information on the status of the hub ports of a 2505 router.
show interface ethernet [interface number]	Shows the current configuration of a specified Ethernet interface.
show interface serial [interface number]	Shows the current configuration of a specified serial interface.
show interfaces	Lists all the interfaces on the router and statistics related to the interface, such as their current configuration and encapsulation. Also tells you whether the interface is active.
show processes	Shows CPU utilization information.
show protocol	Lists the routing protocols configured on the router.
show version	Shows the version of the IOS currently running on the router.
show memory	Displays information about the memory available on the router after the system image loads (show memory free shows only free RAM).

Several of these show commands are revisited throughout the book as you configure router interfaces and other router parameters in the chapters on TCP/IP, IPX/SPX, and WAN Protocols.

Telnet

You can also log in to a router using a virtual terminal connection. This is accomplished by telnetting from a computer or router on the network to the target router. You must know the IP address of one of the interfaces on the target router to log in using Telnet.

Telnetting is possible because of the Telnet protocol. Telnet is a TCP/IP Application layer protocol (the OSI model) that enables you to connect a local computer to a remote device, such as a router or other computer. The local computer becomes a virtual terminal that has access to applications and other resources on the remote device.

Software programs that support Telnet are often referred to as terminal emulation programs, meaning they enable the device to emulate or pretend that it is a dumb terminal connected directly to another device. Telnet is built into the Cisco IOS.

You can telnet to a router from a computer, switch, or router. In addition, when using Telnet on the router, you can telnet from the user or privileged modes. All you would need to know is the Telnet password for the remote router.

To telnet to a router from a router that provides a console connection, follow these steps:

1. At the user mode prompt (or privileged mode prompt—more about the privileged mode in the next section), type **telnet IP Address** (where IP Address is the IP address of one of the target router's interfaces).

2. Type the Virtual Terminal password at the Password prompt.

3. Press Enter to enter the password.

You are then logged in to the remote router (see the following figure). You can now view settings related to the remote router. When you want to log off the remote router, you can type **logout** or **exit** and then press Enter.

```
Alice>telnet 10.2.1.1
Trying 10.2.1.1 ... Open

             ********WELCOME TO SWEETPEA'S ROUTER********

Access Verification

Password:
sweetpea>█
```

After you are logged in to a router via a Telnet session, you can execute any of the CLI commands discussed in this chapter. However, to use commands available only in the privileged mode, such as show running config, you also must know the privileged password for the router to which you have telnetted.

One important point regarding Telnet on a router: You must make sure that the remote router has been configured for a virtual terminal password. Otherwise, you will not be able to telnet to the router.

TAKE THE TEST

This Practice Test provides you with questions related to the IOS CLI Router objective in the "Cisco Basics, IOS & Network Basics" category. This question set also contains questions on the Telnet objective, which is part of the "Network Management" subject category. Because the CCNA exam is in a multiple choice format, these questions, while related to hands-on router commands, are formatted as they would be for the actual test.

1. Which is the global configuration command to enable CDP on a router where it has been disabled?

   A. CDP enable

   B. show CDP

   C. CDP run

   D. run CDP

Answer A is incorrect; enable is not part of the command syntax for enabling CDP on the router. Answer B is incorrect; show CDP is a fragment of an actual command that, with additional parameters, would enable you to view various CDP parameters related to the router. **Answer C is correct; CDP run, executed at the configuration prompt, enables CDP on the router.** Answer D is incorrect; the command words are reversed, providing an incorrect command syntax.

2. Which prompt shows you are in the privileged mode?

   A. router>

   B. router (config)

   C. router#

   D. router (config-if)

Answer A is incorrect; this shows the router in the user mode. Answer B is incorrect; this shows a router in the global configuration mode. **Answer C is correct; it is the privileged prompt that is shown.** Answer D is incorrect; this shows a router in the interface configuration mode.

   3. What are possible avenues for logging in to a router (select all that apply)?

   A. A virtual terminal

   B. The router console

   C. An auxiliary connection through a modem

   D. Configuration session

Answer A is correct; you can telnet to a router using a virtual terminal connection. Answer B is correct; you can directly log in to a router through a router console connection. Answer C is correct; an auxiliary connection through a modem enables you to log in to a router remotely. Answer D is incorrect; you must be logged in to the router before entering a configuration session from the privileged mode.

   4. To get help with the parameters, what you should enter directly after a specific router command at the CLI?

   A. Type the command and follow it with a question mark.

   B. Type **help** and view the command parameters on the help screen.

   C. Type the command, press the spacebar, and type a question mark.

   D. Type a question mark at any prompt.

Answer A is incorrect; this will work only in cases where you want to find the complete command word when a partial command has been typed in. Answer B is incorrect; the help command provides assistance with only how to use help on the router. **Answer C is correct; you must complete a portion of the command (in other words, a whole command word) and then follow it by a space to view additional parameters that follow that command.** Answer D is incorrect; this will show a list of all the commands available at the current prompt.

   5. To view the CDP information for a particular interface type such as Ethernet 0, you would use the command:

   A. `show interface`

   B. `sh cdp int e0`

C. `show cdp interface`

D. `show cdp neighbor`

Answer A is incorrect; this command will provide only interface settings and activity on the interface. **Answer B is correct; the `show cdp int` command followed by a particular interface (such as `e0`) provides CDP information on that specified interface.** Answer C is incorrect; this will show the cdp information for all CDP-enabled interfaces on the router. Answer D is incorrect; the `show cdp neighbor` command provides a listing of CDP neighbors for the router.

6. To view the contents of NVRAM use the command:

A. `show run-config`

B. `show flash`

C. `show startup-config`

D. `show mem`

Answer A is incorrect; this command shows the currently running configuration held in RAM. Answer B is incorrect; this shows the IOS image files held in FLASH RAM. **Answer C is correct; the `show startup-configuration` command shows the startup configuration stored in NVRAM.** Answer D is incorrect; the `show mem` command provides a listing of the items currently held in various memory levels of RAM.

7. Which memory type holds the full IOS image for the router?

A. ROM

B. RAM

C. NVRAM

D. Flash

Answer A is incorrect; ROM holds the bootstrap program and will hold a truncated version of the IOS image (except on the 7000 series routers, where it is a full IOS image). Answer B is incorrect; RAM is used to load portions of the IOS into memory. Answer C is incorrect; NVRAM is used to hold configuration files. **Answer D is correct; the IOS image is typically held and loaded from Flash RAM.**

8. Which command enables you to view recently used commands?

A. `sh history`

B. `set history`

C. `sh protocol`

D. `sh run-config`

Answer A is correct; the `show history` command enables you to see the last 10 CLI commands (by default). Answer B is incorrect; this command is used to set the size of the history file (the number of commands remembered). Answer C is incorrect; `show protocol` is used to view protocol information related to the router. Answer D is incorrect; the `show run` command provides the running configuration contained in RAM.

9. Which command provides information about other directly connected routers?

A. `show ip route`

B. `show cdp neighbor`

C. `show protocol`

D. `sh interface`

Answer A is incorrect; this command provides the IP routing table. **Answer B is correct; `show cdp neighbor` provides information on routers directly connected to the router.** Answer C is incorrect; `show protocol` provides a listing of the protocols being routed on the router. Answer D is incorrect; `show interface` provides interface settings for the router's various interfaces.

10. How do you move the cursor to the beginning of the command line after you've typed a command?

A. Ctrl+B

B. Home

C. Ctrl+F

D. Ctrl+A

Answer A is incorrect; these keys enable you to move one character back. Answer B is incorrect; this keystroke will have no result at the CLI. Answer C is incorrect; this key sequence moves forward one character. **Answer D is correct; use Ctrl+A to move the cursor to the beginning of a typed command on the command-line interface.**

Cheat Sheet

The following are connections to a router:

- Console port
- Auxiliary port via a modem or other device
- Telnet over the network from another device

The router provides several CLI modes:

Mode	Use
User	Basic examination of the router status; limited command set; cannot change configuration.
Privileged	Greater examination of router status and configuration; capability to change router status and enter configuration mode.
Configuration	Enables configuration of global router parameters and the entering of specific configuration information for router interfaces and other settings.
RXBOOT	The ROM monitor mode; enables recovery of router functions when the IOS image can't be found (such as a corrupt IOS image). This mode can also be entered by pressing the Break key on a router console during the first minute of the system bootup (this mode can be used to help recall lost passwords on the router).
Setup	This mode is initiated on a new router or a router that does not have a valid startup configuration. It walks you through the router configuration in the System dialog box.

Help System

Invoked using a ? at the command line:

- ?—Provides a list of all commands at the particular prompt
- ? following a letter or partial command—Supplies all commands that begin with that letter or letters

- ? following a command word—Provides additional parameters for command

help—Provides help on using the help system

Router memory types:

> ROM contains the power-on self test and the bootstrap program for the router.
>
> NVRAM (nonvolatile RAM) stores the startup configuration file for the router.
>
> Flash RAM is used to store the Cisco IOS that runs on your router.
>
> RAM provides the temporary storage of information and holds information such as the current routing table. RAM also holds the currently running router configuration.

Basic Command Summary

Command	Results
enable	Enters the privileged mode using the privileged password from the user mode.
disable	Exits the privileged mode to the user mode.
show running-config	Privileged command that shows the router configuration currently running in RAM.
show startup-config	Privileged command that shows the router configuration stored in the router's NVRAM. It's loaded by the router when the router is rebooted.
show CDP neighbor	Shows the routers that are directly connected to your router by LAN or serial connections.
show CDP neighbor detail	Shows more detailed information on routers directly connected to a router.
show clock	Shows the time and date settings for the router.

Continued

Command	Results
show flash	Shows the IOS file or files contained in the router's Flash RAM and the amount of total Flash RAM and used Flash RAM.
show history	Shows a list of your last 10 commands.
show hub	Shows information on the status of the hub ports of a 2505 router.
show interface ethernet [interface number]	Shows the current configuration of a specified Ethernet interface.
show interface serial [interface number]	Shows the current configuration of a specified serial interface.
show interfaces	Lists all the interfaces on the router and statistics related to the interface, such as their current configuration and encapsulation. Also tells you whether the interface is active.
show processes	Shows CPU utilization information.
show protocol	Lists the routing protocols configured on the router.
show version	Shows the version of the IOS currently running on the router.

Editing Commands

Command Keys	Result
Ctrl+A	Moves the cursor to the beginning of the command line.
Ctrl+E	Moves the cursor to the end of the command line.
Esc+F	Moves the cursor forward one word on the command line.

Command Keys	Result
Esc+B	Moves the cursor back one word on the command line.
Backspace	Moves back one character on the command line, deleting the character to the left of the cursor.
Ctrl+F	Moves forward one character from the cursor.
Ctrl+B	Moves backward one character from the cursor.
Command abbreviation followed by Tab	Completes the abbreviated command (sh becomes show).
Ctrl+P	Same as the up arrow, shows most recent command in History.
Ctrl+N	Same as down arrow, moves backward through the History.

Telnet

Telnet is an Application layer protocol in the TCP/IP stack. It provides a way to connect to a router over the network from another device.

The Cisco IOS—Configuration Commands and Passwords

Cisco has divided its CCNA exam objectives into nine categories. This chapter provides additional IOS commands that fall into the "Cisco Basics, IOS & Network Basics" category under the IOS CLI Router objective. Although this chapter embraces only a subset of the commands you need to know under this objective, router commands are also covered in Chapter 3, "The Cisco IOS—Basic Router Commands," and continue in Chapter 5, "The Cisco IOS—Configuration Files and IOS Images." The following objective has been provided as a separate objective number, but remember that it is part of the IOS CLI Router objective begun in Chapter 3.

- IOS CLI Router—Configuration, Passwords, and Banners

IOS CLI Router—Configuration

Basically, two configuration files exist on a router—the configuration that is currently running in memory and the startup configuration file that is stored in NVRAM. When the router is rebooted, the configuration file in NVRAM is loaded into the router's RAM.

In the last chapter, the show command was explored in relation to the running and startup configuration files. To show the running configuration, use the command show running-config.

Viewing the running-config provides you with a complete picture of the parameters running on the router, which is why it is a privileged mode command. It contains information important to the router's administrator and so is protected by the enable secret password (or the enable password on earlier versions of the IOS).

The backup copy of the running configuration is your startup configuration (although the two files can differ). As you fine-tune your running configuration, a time will come when you want to save it to NVRAM as the startup configuration. The great thing about the copy command is that you can copy information from RAM to NVRAM (running to startup) or vice versa.

To copy the running configuration to the startup configuration file in NVRAM (the current startup configuration file will be overwritten), follow these steps:

1. If you are at the User prompt, type **enable** and press Enter.

2. Supply the enable password, and then press Enter.

3. In the privileged mode (achieved with steps 1 and 2), type **copy running config startup-config**. Press Enter to execute the command.

The router will let you know that it is "building configuration." It will then output [OK] when the copy process is complete (see the following figure).

If you use the show command to view the running and startup configuration, you will find that they are now identical.

If you find yourself in a situation where you have been modifying the running configuration and the router doesn't seem to be operating correctly, you can copy the startup configuration into RAM, replacing the running configuration. However, you'll lose any changes you've made to the running configuration. To do this, type `copy startup-config running-config` at the privileged prompt, and then press Enter. The router lets you know that the router has been configured from memory, meaning the running configuration has been replaced by the startup configuration.

Remember that commands can be abbreviated; `copy run start` is the same as `copy running-config startup-config`. Don't let abbreviated commands confuse you on the exam.

Additionally, the only way you can really get comfortable with abbreviated commands is to actually practice abbreviating commands on the router. When you abbreviate a command to the point where the router can't tell it from another command or commands, you will get the ambiguous command message at the router prompt.

For example, if I type `c run start` (an abbreviated version of the `copy run start` command), the router will return the ambiguous command message because it doesn't know whether I want the command `copy`, `configure`, or `connect`; they all begin with the letter "c" (even though I wouldn't use `configure` or `connect` followed by `run start`).

You can also erase the contents of NVRAM, but only if you want to either immediately copy the running configuration to the NVRAM or reload the router and set up the router's configuration as if it were a new router. At the privileged prompt, type `erase startup-config`, and then press Enter. The startup configuration will be erased. If you now turn off the router or use the `reload` command, the router enters the initial configuration dialog about booting up.

Router Passwords

When you create an initial configuration (discussed in this chapter) for your router, you are prompted to supply router passwords and a hostname for the router (as well as a lot of other information, such as which network protocols you want to route and which interfaces you want to enable). You also can configure these items on the router in the configuration mode. The configuration mode is entered via the privileged mode.

The configuration mode enables you to set all the parameters related to the hardware and software running on the router. You can configure interfaces, routed protocols, and routing protocols. The bottom line is that the configuration mode gives you access to absolutely all the commands you would use to configure or fine-tune the configuration for the router.

Setting Router Passwords and the Hostname

When you configure the router using the initial configuration dialog (discussed later in this chapter), you set router passwords such as the enable secret password, enable password, and virtual terminal password. You are also given the option of setting a hostname for the router (the name that appears to the left of the prompt on the command-line interface).

You also can set these router parameters using the configuration mode (and set other passwords, such as the login password for the router). Some confusion results from the fact that an enable secret password and an enable password exist. The enable secret password is an encrypted password used to enter the privileged mode on the router. It is supported by IOS version 10.3 and greater and takes precedence over the enable password (if the enable secret password has been set on the router).

The enable password is used on routers running earlier versions of the IOS (earlier than 10.3). When you set the enable secret password and the enable password, they cannot be the same, so remember that the enable secret password is the password you will actually use to gain access to the router's privileged mode.

To set the enable secret password on the router, follow these steps:

1. Enter the privileged mode on the router using the `enable` command.

2. At the privileged prompt, type `config t` and press Enter.

3. At the configuration prompt, type **enable secret *password***, where *password* is the password you want to use. Then press Enter.

4. Press Ctrl+Z to exit the configuration mode.

You are then returned to the privileged prompt. Exit the privileged prompt by typing **disable** and pressing Enter. Now, use the enable command and your new secret password to enter the privileged mode.

Other passwords can be set on the router related to virtual terminal connections and login to the router. Table 4.1 summarizes these global configuration commands.

Table 4.1   Other Router Passwords

Password	Configuration Command	Purpose
Enable	enable *password*	This sets the enable password. Only used on routers that do not have a secret enable password or are using IOS versions earlier than 10.3.
Login	line con 0 [enter] login [enter] password *password*	This password controls login to the router from the console.
Virtual Terminal	line vty 0 4 [enter] password *password*	This password controls virtual terminal logins to the router. The 0 4 following vty means that five telnet sessions are allowed.

The following figure shows these commands as they would be executed on the router in the configuration mode.

```
Tera Term - COM1 VT                                          _ ◻ ✕
File  Edit  Setup  Control  Window  Help
sweetpea#config t
Enter configuration commands, one per line.  End with CNTL/Z.
sweetpea(config)#enable secret hahraken
sweetpea(config)#line con 0
sweetpea(config-line)#login
sweetpea(config-line)#password joseph
sweetpea(config-line)#line vty 0 4
sweetpea(config-line)#password cisco
sweetpea(config-line)#^Z
sweetpea#
4d23h: %SYS-5-CONFIG_I: Configured from console by console
sweetpea#
```

Another global configuration command is the hostname command, which enables you to set the name of the router. At the configuration prompt, type **hostname** *name*, where *name* is the name you want to assign the router. After pressing Enter, use Ctrl+Z to end your configuration session (see the following figure).

```
Tera Term - COM1 VT                                          _ ◻ ✕
File  Edit  Setup  Control  Window  Help
Alice#config t
Enter configuration commands, one per line.  End with CNTL/Z.
Alice(config)#hostname wimpy
wimpy(config)#^Z
wimpy#
%SYS-5-CONFIG_I: Configured from console by console
wimpy#
```

After making changes to the router's running configuration, be sure you use copy run start at the privileged prompt to make these changes part of the startup configuration. Otherwise, all your changes will be lost if the router is rebooted or loses power.

Router Banners

You can create a message-of-the-day (motd) banner that will be displayed any time someone logs in to the router. The router banner is created in the configuration mode. The command you use is banner motd *end character*, where *end character* is a keyboard character of your choice that tells the configuration mode when you have completed your banner text. For example, you will want to choose a character such as the number sign (#), dollar sign ($), or other character that will not appear in the body of your banner (such as most letters of the alphabet). Follow these steps:

1. At the privileged prompt, type **config terminal**. You are placed in the configuration mode with the console (terminal is the source for the configuration information).

2. We will use the dollar sign ($) as our end character, so type **banner motd $**. Then, press Enter. Next, you will be told to type your banner text and end the banner with the $ character.

3. Type the text for your banner. Use the Enter key to place blank lines in the banner text, and use the spacebar to position items from left to right in the banner. The following figure shows a sample router banner.

4. Type your selected end character ($ in this case) and press Enter. You will be returned to the configuration mode.

5. Press Ctrl+Z to save your banner and exit the configuration mode.

After exiting the configuration mode, you might have to press Enter once to return to the privileged prompt. To view your router banner, type **quit** and press Enter. This exits you from the router. When you press Enter on the initial router screen, your router banner will appear. If you have set up the router with a login password, you will be asked to provide the password to enter the router.

Other router banner types are also available (although on the CCNA exam you will most likely be asked about motd banners only, but it's not a bad idea to know about the other banner types). Table 4.2 shows these banner types, the configuration commands to create them, and the purposes of the banners.

Table 4.2 Other Router Banners

Banner	Configuration Command	Purpose
Line Activation	`banner exec message` `[end character such` `as #]`	This message is displayed when an incoming connection is initiated, such as a virtual terminal line.
Idle Terminal	`vacant-message message` `[end character such` `as #]`	This message is displayed on a console that is not in use.

71

Table 4.2   continued

Banner	Configuration Command	Purpose

Host Failed	`busy-message hostname`
	`message [end`
	`character such as #]`
		This message is displayed when an attempt to connect to a particular hostname (supplied as the hostname parameter) fails.

Understanding the Router Startup

The router startup is dependant on the configuration register and the boot command in determining where the router will find the IOS image it is to load and its startup configuration file. When special parameters are related to the IOS image or startup configuration (which normally load from Flash and NVRAM, respectively), the normal boot procedure is as follows:

- When you power the router on, the ROM chip runs a power-on self test (POST) that checks the router's hardware, such as the processor, interfaces, and memory. This test is not unlike the power-on test that a PC runs when you power it on (RAM, CPU, and other hardware is checked).

- The next step in the router bootup sequence is the execution of a bootstrap program stored in the router's ROM. This bootstrap program performs a search for the CISCO IOS. The IOS can be loaded from the ROM itself (if no valid IOS image is found—routers either have a partial or complete copy of the CISCO IOS in ROM), the router's FLASH RAM, or a TFTP server on the network.

- After the router's IOS is loaded, the router searches for the router's configuration file. The configuration file is normally held in NVRAM (a copy command is used to copy a running configuration to NVRAM). As with the IOS, however, the configuration file can be loaded from a TFTP server (again, the location of the configuration file would be dictated by information held in the router's ROM registry).

- After the router loads the configuration file, the information in the file enables the interfaces and provides parameters related to routed and routing protocols in force on the router. Keep in mind that loading the

IOS from a source other than Flash RAM requires a notation in the ROM's configuration registry and that, to load the configuration file from a source other than NVRAM, information pointing to the location of the file must be contained in NVRAM.

If the router can't find a valid IOS image, or if the boot sequence is interrupted, you will be dumped in the ROM monitor mode. Within the first six seconds, you can interrupt the boot sequence yourself by using the reload command at the privileged prompt and then executing the break sequence for your terminal emulation software—typically Break or Alt+B. On the other hand, you can quickly get your router up and running by using the boot command at the ROM monitor prompt.

Examples of using the boot command in the ROM monitor mode follow:

- boot *IOS filename ip address*—This boot command enables you to load the IOS by specifying a filename and the IP address of the TFTP server that holds the file.

- boot flash *filename*—This boot command enables you to load an alternative IOS image from Flash in cases where your Flash RAM holds more than one IOS image.

- boot flash *partition number filename*—This boot command enables you to load an IOS image stored in a particular Flash partition (this command is particular to the 1600, 2500, 2600, and 3600 series routers where you can partition your Flash RAM—the global configuration command is partition size1 size2, where the size is the number of bytes and the number specifies the partition; the two parameters are separated by a space).

As soon as you enter one of the previously listed commands and press Enter, your router reboots and looks for the IOS image at the location you specified. This is an excellent way to get your router on its feet when the IOS image in Flash has become corrupted. Then, after the router is up, you can copy a new image into Flash or another location (wherever you boot the IOS from).

Don't get the boot command used at the ROM monitor prompt confused with the boot system command, which is used at the configuration prompt. The boot system command enables you to specify different locations to boot the IOS from and is discussed in the next chapter.

At the CCNA level, you aren't expected to do a lot in the ROM monitor mode. However, you do need to know the boot sequence, and you should understand how you can use the boot command at the ROM monitor prompt. Don't experiment too much and mess up your router, but do be sure you understand that alternative sources of the IOS image can be specified for the boot sequence.

The setup Command

When you boot up a new router (or boot a router where the configuration file has been deleted using the privileged command erase startup-config), the system configuration dialog is loaded. You also can enter the initial configuration dialog by entering the setup command at the privileged prompt.

This setup mode asks you a series of questions; the answers to those questions provide a basic configuration for the router.

To reload a router where you have erased the startup configuration, use the reload command, and then press Enter to confirm the reload. The router reboots and the system configuration dialog appears on the router console screen.

Working through the setup dialog is very straightforward. The router asks you a question and you supply the appropriate parameter, such as the IP address for a particular interface or the routing protocols you want to run on the router. This is why they call this process the setup dialog; you are having a dialog with the router. The configuration dialog first supplies a summary of the interfaces on the router and their current statuses.

The following steps summarize the information you are asked to provide by the initial configuration dialog on a Cisco 2505 router running Cisco IOS 11.3. This version of the IOS supports IP, IPX, AppleTalk, and DECnet routing.

1. After supplying you with an interface summary, the setup dialog asks you to provide a router hostname. Type the hostname and press Enter.

2. The next setup dialog question asks you to provide an enable secret password. Type an appropriate password, and then press Enter.

3. You are then asked to provide an enable password (which is necessary only for earlier versions of the IOS). Enter a password other than the enable secret password and press Enter.

4. You are asked to provide a virtual terminal password. Provide the password and press Enter to continue.

5. The next setup dialog question asks you whether you want to enable *Simple Network Management Protocol* (SNMP). This protocol provides baselines for network operations and provides a way to monitor changes in the network using a management station, which requires software such as CiscoWorks. If you want to enable SNMP, press Enter. The default community string is public. Press Enter to use this community or enter your own.

6. You are queried about the network protocols you want to route on the network. A default answer (no or yes) is provided as each protocol is listed. Enable the protocols, such as IPX and IP, that you want to route.

7. The next series of questions relates to the routing protocols you want to use. If you are routing IP then IGRP and RIP can be enabled. If you enable IGRP, you are also asked to provide an autonomous system number (more about IGRP is covered in Chapter 8, "Internetwork Routing").

8. Finally, you are given the opportunity to enable LAN interfaces on the router, such as Ethernet, Token Ring, FDDI, ISDN, and serial interfaces. You are asked whether the interface is in use (answer yes if it is). Then, if you are routing IP on the router, you are asked to supply the IP address and the subnet bits for each interface (more about IP addresses and subnet bits is discussed in Chapter 6, "Network Protocols—TCP/IP").

After enabling the various interfaces, you are asked whether you want to use this configuration. If you answer yes, the configuration is saved to NVRAM as the startup configuration and loaded into RAM as the current running configuration. The following figure shows the initial configuration dialog for a 2505 router.

```
Tera Term - COM2 VT
File Edit Setup Control Window Help
Configuring global parameters:

  Enter host name [Router]: popeye

The enable secret is a one-way cryptographic secret used
instead of the enable password when it exists.

  Enter enable secret: spinach

The enable password is used when there is no enable secret
and when using older software and some boot images.

  Enter enable password: cisco
  Enter virtual terminal password: bluto
  Configure SNMP Network Management? [yes]:
    Community string [public]:
  Configure DECnet? [no]:
  Configure AppleTalk? [no]:
  Configure IPX? [no]:
  Configure IP? [yes]:
    Configure IGRP routing? [yes]:
    Your IGRP autonomous system number [1]:

Configuring interface parameters:

Configuring interface Ethernet0:
  Is this interface in use? [yes]:
  Configure IP on this interface? [yes]:
    IP address for this interface: 10.7.1.1
    Number of bits in subnet field [0]: 8
    Class A network is 10.0.0.0, 8 subnet bits; mask is /16
  Enable all hub ports on this interface? [yes]:

Configuring interface Serial0:
  Is this interface in use? [yes]:
  Configure IP on this interface? [yes]:
  Configure IP unnumbered on this interface? [no]:
    IP address for this interface: 10.8.1.1
    Number of bits in subnet field [8]:
    Class A network is 10.0.0.0, 8 subnet bits; mask is /16

Configuring interface Serial1:
  Is this interface in use? [yes]:
```

You will find that the initial configuration does not enable you to configure WAN protocols and other parameters related to serial interfaces. These parameters must be entered in the interface configuration mode. More about WAN protocols and configuring WAN protocols on serial interfaces is covered in Chapters 9, "WAN Protocols—HDLC Frame Relay and ATM," and 10, "WAN Protocols—Configuring PPP and ISDN."

Enabling IP Routing

During the initial configuration of your router, you enable IP by answering yes when you're asked to "Configure IP." IP routing can also be enabled on the router at the configuration prompt when you type **ip routing** and press Enter.

To actually route IP on your router, however, you must configure router interfaces with IP addresses and enable a routing protocol, such as RIP or IGRP, on the router. Configuring router interfaces with IP addresses can be accomplished during the initial configuration by supplying the IP address for a particular interface and the number of subnet bits (*subnet bits* refers to the number of bits you have used to create the subnets on your network). Interfaces also can be configured with IP addresses and subnet masks in the interface configuration mode (which differs from the global configuration mode that we have worked in so far). For example, to configure the Ethernet 0 interface, at the configuration prompt, you would type **interface Ethernet 0** and press Enter. This changes the configuration prompt to config-if. This means that you can now enter configuration information specific to that interface. Configuring router interfaces with IP addresses is covered in Chapter 6 in the "Configure IP Addresses" section.

TAKE THE TEST

This Practice Test provides you with questions related to the IOS CLI Router objective found in the "Cisco Basics, IOS & Network Basics" category of the CCNA exam outline. Because the CCNA exam is in a multiple choice format, these questions are formatted as they would be on the actual exam.

1. When is the enable password used (select all that apply)?

   A. On routers where a secret enable password does not exist

   B. On routers running an IOS earlier than 10.3

   C. Never

   D. To log in to a telnet session

Answer A is correct; the enable password is in force when a secret enable has not been configured. Answer B is correct; only the enable password is supported by earlier versions of the IOS. Answer C is incorrect; two cases (as stated in A and B) exist in which the enable password is used. Answer D is incorrect; the virtual terminal password is used to log in to a telnet session on a router.

2. How do you copy the router configuration in RAM to NVRAM?

   A. `copy start run`

   B. `copy run start`

   C. `copy mem`

   D. `copy RAM NVRAM`

Answer A is incorrect; this command copies the configuration in NVRAM to RAM. **Answer B is correct; `copy run start` is the abbreviated version of `copy running-config startup-config`, which copies from RAM to NVRAM.** Answer C is incorrect; `copy mem` is not an existing command. `write` mem was used in earlier versions of the ISO to copy from RAM to NVRAM. Answer D is incorrect; RAM and NVRAM do not provide appropriate syntax for the copy command.

3. What is the configuration command to set the encrypted password for the router?

   A. `router password password`

   B. `enable login password password`

   C. `enable secret password password`

   D. `line con 0 password`

Answer A is incorrect; the syntax for the password command is incorrect. Answer B is incorrect; `enable` is not used with the login and password commands to set a password. **Answer C is correct; the command is `secret password` followed by the password you want to use.** Answer D is incorrect; the syntax for the password command is incorrect.

4. What is the correct configuration command to begin the process of creating a message of the day banner on the router?

   A. `write banner`

   B. `banner #`

   C. `motd banner #`

   D. `banner motd #`

Answer A is incorrect; the `write` command is not used to create a banner. Answer B is incorrect; the `banner configuration` command is incomplete. Answer C is incorrect; the command is not written in the correct order. **Answer D is correct; the command is `banner motd` followed by an end text character.**

5. What is the configuration command for changing the name of the router?

   A. `router name name`

   B. `hostname name`

   C. `line console name`

   D. `host name name`

Answer A is incorrect; there is no `router name` command. **Answer B is correct; the `hostname` command followed by the actual name is the correct configuration command.** Answer C is incorrect; you do not name the line console. Answer D is incorrect; there is a space between `host` and `name` on the command line.

6. What is the global configuration command for enabling IP routing on the router?

A. `ip protocol`

B. `enable ip`

C. `ip routing`

D. `route ip`

Answer A is incorrect; `ip protocol` is not a configuration command. Answer B is incorrect; the `enable` command is not used to enable IP routing. **Answer C is correct; `ip routing` is used at the configuration prompt to enable the routing of IP.** Answer D is incorrect; `route ip` is an erroneous command.

7. What is the privileged command that can be used to enter the initial configuration dialog without erasing the current configuration?

A. `setup`

B. `reload`

C. `copy start run`

D. `erase start`

Answer A is correct; you can enter the initial configuration dialog by using the `setup` command. Answer B is incorrect; `reload` is actually used to restart the router. Answer C is incorrect; this is the command to copy the startup configuration to the running configuration. Answer D is incorrect; it is the command used to erase the startup configuration from NVRAM.

8. When the router is rebooted, the configuration for the file is loaded from

A. ROM

B. NVRAM

C. Flash

D. RAM

Answer A is incorrect; ROM supplies the POST test and IOS if necessary. **Answer B is correct; the startup configuration file is typically stored in NVRAM.** Answer C is incorrect; the IOS is typically stored in Flash. Answer D is incorrect; the RAM is flushed when the router is rebooted.

9. What are the series of commands (commands are separated by commas) to change your telnet password for the router to Cisco?

   A. config t, line con 0, login, password cisco

   B. config t, enable password cisco

   C. config t, line vty 0 4, login, telnet cisco

   D. configt t, line vty 0 4, login, password cisco

Answer A is incorrect; it is the command to configure a router login password. Answer B is incorrect; it is the command for a router's enable password. Answer C is incorrect; telnet is not part of the configuration line syntax for creating a telnet password. **Answer D is correct; you must enter the configuration mode, specify the virtual terminal line (line vty 0 4), and then specify that you want to set the login password.**

Cheat Sheet

To view the running configuration, use the show running-config command at the privileged prompt.

To copy the running configuration to NVRAM, use the copy running config startup-config command at the privileged prompt.

To copy the startup configuration to RAM, use the copy startup-config running-config command at the privileged prompt.

To erase the startup configuration and reboot the router, use the erase startup-config command followed by the reload command (at the privileged prompt).

To set the encrypted router password, use enable secret *password* at the configuration prompt.

To set other router passwords at the configuration prompt, use the following:

Password	Configuration Command
Enable	enable *password*
Login	line con 0 [enter] login [enter]password *password*
Virtual Terminal	line vty 0 4 [enter] password *password*

Use the hostname *name* command at the configuration prompt to set the router's name.

If a router is incapable of finding a valid IOS image, use the boot command at the ROM monitor prompt to specify the image the router should use to boot.

To create a banner that will appear when someone logs in to the router, use the banner motd # command at the configuration prompt. The # character is used when you have finished entering the text for your banner.

The privileged setup command can be used to enter the initial configuration dialog. Network protocols can be enabled, such as IP routing, during the initial configuration.

The global configuration command ip routing turns on the routing of IP on the router.

The Cisco IOS—Configuration Files and IOS Images

Cisco has divided its CCNA exam objectives into nine categories. This chapter provides additional IOS commands that fall into the Cisco "Basics, IOS & Network Basics" category under the IOS CLI Router objective. This chapter embraces only a subset of the commands you need to know under this objective. Other router commands are covered in Chapters 3, "The Cisco IOS— Basic Router Commands," and 4, "The Cisco IOS—Configuration Commands and Passwords." Although this subject matter falls under the IOS CLI Router objective introduced in Chapter 3, the objective has been given a sequence number for clarity as shown below.

- IOS CLI Router—copying, storing, and manipulating configuration and IOS files.

13

IOS CLI Router—Configuration and IOS File Manipulation

You already learned in the last chapter that two configuration files exist on your router: the running configuration, which is currently running in the router's RAM, and the startup configuration, which is stored in NVRAM. You can use the command `copy running-config startup-config` to copy the running configuration to NVRAM. This overwrites the existing copy of the startup configuration that is in NVRAM (Chapter 4 also discusses copying the startup configuration to RAM using `copy start run`).

You can also manipulate the configuration that is running in RAM or the configuration file that is stored in NVRAM by copying these configurations to a TFTP server (in essence, backing up the particular configuration) or copying a configuration file from the TFTP server. In the latter case, you can copy to RAM and replace the running configuration or copy to NVRAM to replace the startup configuration.

Not only can you copy your startup configuration to a TFTP server, but you can also configure the router so that the location of the startup configuration that should be loaded is specified (a location other than NVRAM). This is accomplished using the global configuration command `boot host`. This command can be used to load the configuration file from a couple different locations.

- `boot host mop` *file name* *mac-address* enables you to boot a configuration file from a DEC mop server (a server running the Maintenance Operation Protocol). The interface on the router that is on the same network as the mop server must be mop-enabled using the `mop enable` command.

- `boot host tftp` *file name* *ip address* loads the configuration file specified with the filename on a TFTP server with the specified IP address (more about TFTP later in this chapter). The configuration commands no boot host mop and no boot host tftp disable the loading of a configuration file from a remote source.

Before you can load the configuration files from an alternative location, you must be able to copy the configuration file to that location (such as a TFTP server). The next section takes a look at using TFTP servers.

The Trivial File Transport Protocol

Trivial File Transfer Protocol (TFTP) is a TCP/IP Application layer protocol that can be used to move files from the router to a PC running TFTP server software. TFTP is actually similar to the File Transfer Protocol (FTP) that is used for uploading and downloading files on the Internet.

Unlike FTP, however, TFTP does not require a username or password to log on to a server (hence the "trivial" notation). All you need to know is the IP address of the computer running the TFTP server software, and you can copy your configuration file to the server.

You also can use TFTP servers to copy a configuration file to your router or upgrade (or change) your router IOS image by copying a new IOS file to the router's flash RAM. Because routers do not have disk drives, TFTP servers provide you with an alternative location for backup files related to the router (such as a copy of the configuration or alternative configurations). So, a TFTP server is any PC that is running TFTP server software and is accessible on the network.

Copying Configuration Files to the TFTP Server

To copy your startup configuration to a TFTP server, start the TFTP server software that you use on the appropriate server or workstation computer. (The TFTP server must be on the network and be configured for TCP/IP with a valid subnet mask, IP address, and default gateway address.)

After the TFTP server is up and running (ping the TFTP server from the router to make sure), you are ready to copy the configuration file to the TFTP server:

1. On your router console, enter the privileged mode using the enable command and the enable password.

2. At the router prompt, type **copy startup-config tftp**, and then press Enter.

3. You are asked to provide the IP address of the remote host. Enter the IP address of the TFTP server (in this case the IP address used was 10.16.0.4). Then, press Enter.

4. You will be asked to supply the name of the file you want to write to the server. The default is the router's name followed by config (such as cisco2505-config). Press Enter to accept the default or enter the name of the configuration file you want to copy, and then press Enter.

5. You will then be asked to confirm the procedure (see the following figure).

6. Press Enter to confirm.

The file will be written to the TFTP server. A prompt saying Writing router name-config. !! [OK] means that the copy was a success. If you return to the TFTP Server workstation and look at the server window, you will find that a record of the copy job has been recorded on your TFTP server.

You also can copy the running-config from RAM using the procedure outlined. The only difference is that the command in step 2 would instead read copy running-config tftp.

Copying from the TFTP Server

The reverse operation—copying a file from the TFTP server to the router—is as straightforward as the process outlined in the previous section. You can copy a configuration file from the TFTP server into the router's NVRAM or you can copy the configuration from the server directly into RAM as a new running configuration. If you copy the file into NVRAM, it not only becomes the new running configuration for the router but it also will be the startup configuration when you reboot the router. Make sure that the configuration file on the TFTP server is in the same folder as the TFTP server software. Follow these steps:

1. Start the TFTP server software on the server workstation.

2. On your router console, enter the privileged mode using the enable command and the enable password.

3. At the router prompt type **copy tftp startup-config**, and then press Enter.

4. You are asked to provide the IP address of the remote host. Enter the IP address of the TFTP server (in this case the IP address was 10.16.0.4). Then, press Enter.

5. You are asked to provide the name of the configuration file on the TFTP server you want to copy. Type the name at the prompt (if you use the default name when you copied the file to the server, you do not need to enter a new name). Press Enter to continue.

6. You will be asked to confirm the procedure (see the following figure).

7. Press Enter to confirm.

The file is loaded to the router and becomes the active configuration (and is saved in NVRAM). Again, you will receive an [OK] message on the router that the procedure was a success. You can return to the TFTP server, where the process will also be confirmed as a success.

You also can copy a running configuration from the TFTP server using the command copy tftp run. This places the configuration file directly into RAM.

An alternative to using the copy tftp command (in copying configurations to both the running and startup configurations) is to use the config command. For example, to copy a new configuration directly into the router's RAM (a new running configuration), use the command config net and then press Enter. You are then asked to supply the IP address of the TFTP server. After pressing Enter again, you are asked to supply the name of the configuration file. After confirming that the router will be configured with this new configuration, you are provided with a prompt that the configuration is loading.

You can also use a form of the config command to overwrite the startup configuration in NVRAM. Use the command config overwrite-network, and then supply the IP address of the TFTP server and the name of the configuration file. This enables you to place a different startup configuration on the router just as the copy tftp start command does.

Loading the Cisco IOS

Chapter 4 discussed the ROM Monitor mode boot command that is used as a last ditch effort to specify the location of the router's IOS. From a more practical standpoint (meaning you expect the router to boot normally), you might want to specify alternative IOS loading strategies (loading the IOS from places other than the router's Flash RAM) in your router's startup configuration. You can use the global configuration boot system command and specify from where you want the router to load the IOS. This enables you to save this configuration information as part of the startup configuration.

The router's search for the IOS image is based on the values in the configuration register. This register is a 16-bit entity represented in hexadecimal format and displayed as 0x210X, where the last digit (the X) is the boot field. The boot field tells you where the router will look for the IOS image. For example, if the configuration register is 0x2100, the router will boot from ROM.

If the register is 0x2101, the router will boot from the IOS subset contained in the router's ROM. If the register is 0x2102 through 0x210F (where the boot field is the hexadecimal character 2–F), the router will use the startup configuration file and the boot parameters you have placed in it to locate and load the IOS file.

The big question is, "What command enables you to see the register?" The answer is the show version command (executed at the user or privileged prompt). The following figure shows the results of the show version command.

The configuration register for the router is 0x2102, which means the startup configuration dictates where the router should look for the IOS. This particular router boots the IOS from Flash (the default configuration for a router).

You can choose to have the router load the IOS from several locations using the boot system configuration command. You can also "stack" the locations using the boot system command so that the router will move down through a list of alternatives until it finds a valid IOS image. The following figure shows an example that configures the router to boot from an image specified in Flash and then an image on a TFTP server if the first load fails.

Table 5.1 summarizes the parameters you can use with the boot system command to specify the location of an IOS image.

Table 5.1 boot system Parameters

Command Syntax	IOS Image Location
boot system flash	Loads image from Flash
boot system flash *filename*	Loads a specific image from Flash
boot system mop *filename mac-address*	Loads a file from a DECnet MOP server
boot system rom	Loads the IOS image in ROM
boot system tftp *image name IP address*	Loads a specific IOS image from a TFTP server (you must specify the IP address of the TFTP server)

The following figure shows a portion of the running configuration for a router that has been configured to boot an IOS image in Flash and, if this load fails, to load the same image from a TFTP server.

The image on the TFTP server is basically serving as a backup from the image that is in Flash. The show run command was used to produce this screen.

Manipulating the IOS Software Image

A TFTP server provides an excellent repository for a backup of your current IOS image and new IOS images you want to upgrade the router with. You can copy the current IOS image to the TFTP server and then copy the image from the TFTP server if a problem occurs when the router attempts to load the IOS from Flash.

You also can use a TFTP server to upgrade your router's IOS. Cisco is constantly fine-tuning the IOS available for its routers. At the time this book was being written, a new release—version 12—became available (and several updates for 12 have already been released by Cisco). Although the current CCNA exam covers IOS 11.2, you will no doubt work with newer IOS versions during your routing career.

Backing Up the Current IOS Image

The copy command is used to copy the router's IOS image (from Flash) to the TFTP server. You must have your TFTP server online and the TFTP server software running to accomplish this task. Before you start the copy process, you might want to ping the TFTP server to make sure it is reachable. Use ping *IP address*, where *IP address* is the address of the TFTP server. Follow these steps:

1. At the privileged prompt, type **copy flash tftp**, and then press Enter.

2. You are asked to provide the address of the TFTP server (the IP address). Type the IP address and press Enter.

3. Next, you are asked to provide the filename of the IOS. Type the IOS image you want to back up (it was displayed when you initiated the command in step 1; multiple IOS images in Flash should be listed). Then, press Enter.

4. You will be asked to provide a destination name for the file. To use the default destination, press Enter.

5. To verify the copy, type **y** (for yes) and then press Enter.

The copy from Flash to the TFTP server then takes place. The following figure shows the process on a Cisco 1005 router that uses a PCMCIA card for Flash RAM.

```
Tera Term - COM1 VT
File Edit Setup Control Window Help

Alice#copy flash tftp

PCMCIA flash directory:
File  Length    Name/status
  1   1207924   cpai005-ny-mz_111-24.bin
[1207984tes used, 889164 available, 2097152 total]
Address or name of remote host [10.1.1.3]? 10.1.1.3
Source file name? cpai005-ny-mz_111-24.bin
Destination file name [cpai005-ny-mz_111-24.bin]?
Verifying checksum for 'cpai005-ny-mz_111-24.bin' (file # 1)  OK
Copy 'cpai005-ny-mz_111-24.bin' from Flash to server
  as 'cpai005-ny-mz_111-24.bin'? [yes/no]y
!!!!!!!!!!!!!!!!!!!!!!!!!!!!!!!!!!!!!!!!!!!!!!!!!!!!!!!!!!!!!!!!!!!!!!!!!!!!!!!!!!!!!!!!!
!!!!!!!!!!!!!!!!!!!!!!!!!!!!!!!!!!!!!!!!!!!!!!!!!!!!!!!!!!!!!!!!!!!!!!!!!!!!!!!!!!!!!!!!!
Upload to server done
Flash copy took 00:00:44 [hh:mm:ss]
Alice#
```

Copying an IOS Image from the TFTP Server

To copy an IOS image from a TFTP server to Flash, you use the command copy tftp flash. This command can be used to replace an IOS image that has become corrupted or to place an IOS image in Flash that has been erased (Flash can be erased with the command erase flash). This command is also used when you want to upgrade the IOS version on the router:

1. On your router console, enter the privileged mode using the enable command and the enable password.

2. At the router prompt, type **copy tftp flash**, and then press Enter.

3. You are notified that the router will proceed with the copy but that router functions will be ended while the IOS image is updated. Press Enter to confirm.

4. Next, you are asked to provide the IP address of the remote host. Enter the IP address of the TFTP server (in this case, the IP address was 10.16.0.4). Press Enter.

5. You are asked to provide the name of the IOS file on the TFTP server you want to copy. Type the name at the prompt (make sure that the file is an IOS image; 80114109.bin is an image for IOS 11.2). Press Enter to continue.

6. You are then asked for the destination filename. Go with the default name of the IOS (as entered in step 5). Press Enter to continue.

7. Next, you are asked to confirm that the Flash RAM will be erased before the new IOS is written to it. Press Enter to confirm. Because Flash contains the current IOS, you will be asked to confirm a second time. Press Enter to confirm.

8. You are then asked whether you want to save the modified system configuration. Type **Yes** and press Enter. You can see the entries on a 2505 router for the upgrade of the IOS in the following figure.

9. You are asked for a final confirmation to proceed with the Flash erase. Type **yes** and press Enter.

The current IOS image is erased and replaced by the new IOS image. A series of exclamation points appears on the router as the process takes place. This process might take a couple of minutes because the IOS images can be quite large (the 11.2 IOS is more than 6 megabytes).

The router reboots after the new IOS file is copied. To check your new IOS image, type show flash at the EXEC prompt, and then press Enter. The new IOS image (the filename you entered in step 6) should now reside in the router's Flash. You can also use the show version command to verify the version of the IOS currently loaded on the router.

TAKE THE TEST

This Practice Test provides you with questions related to the IOS CLI Router objective in the Cisco "Basics, IOS & Network Basics" category. Because the CCNA exam is in a multiple choice format, these questions are formatted as they would be on the actual exam.

1. Which command initiates a copy from NVRAM to a TFTP server?

  A. `copy run tftp`

  B. `copy NVRAM tftp`

  C. `copy start tftp`

  D. `copy tftp start`

Answer A is incorrect; this command copies the running configuration (in RAM) to the TFTP server. Answer B is incorrect; the command syntax is wrong (in other words, NVRAM). **Answer C is correct; the command `copy start tftp` initiates the copying of the contents of NVRAM to a TFTP server.** Answer D is incorrect; this command copies the startup configuration from the TFTP server to NVRAM.

2. Routers can boot the IOS from (select all that apply):

  A. A TFTP server

  B. NVRAM

  C. ROM

  D. Flash RAM

Answer A is correct; a router can boot the IOS from a TFTP server. Answer B is incorrect; the IOS won't fit in NVRAM. **Answer C is correct; ROM either contains a partial or complete IOS image. Answer D is correct; Flash is the typical receptacle for the router's IOS.**

3. To copy a configuration file or IOS image to a TFTP server, you must know the TFTP server's

   A. NetBIOS name

   B. MAC hardware address

   C. IPX address

   D. IP address

Answer A is incorrect; the NetBIOS name will not supply the information to reach the TFTP server (unless the router has been configured to relate NetBIOS names to IP addresses or a DNS server is available). Answer B is incorrect; MAC hardware addresses cannot be used to specify a TFTP server's location. Answer C is incorrect; TFTP cannot relate to IPX addresses (it is a TCP/IP protocol). **Answer D is correct; the IP address is typically used to specify the TFTP server's address.**

4. The boot system command is entered in which mode?

   A. User

   B. Privileged

   C. Configuration

   D. ROM Monitor

Answer A is incorrect; you can't enter configuration commands in the user mode. Answer B is incorrect; you can't enter configuration commands at the privileged prompt. **Answer C is correct; the boot system command is a global configuration command.** Answer D is incorrect; the ROM Monitor mode uses the boot command to specify a manual booting of the IOS but does not use the syntax boot system or enable you to save boot parameters to the router's configuration.

5. Which command enables you to see the current configuration register setting?

   A. show run

   B. show ver

   C. boot system flash

   D. show start

Answer A is incorrect; it shows the running configuration, which does not provide the register setting. **Answer B is correct; the show version command provides the current configuration setting register.** Answer C is incorrect; the `boot system flash` command is a configuration command that configures the router to boot from Flash. Answer D is incorrect; the `show start` command shows the router's startup configuration.

6. Which command enables you to load a new IOS image on the router?

A. `copy tftp start`

B. `copy tftp flash`

C. `copy tftp run`

D. `copy tftp ROM`

Answer A is incorrect; this command enables you to copy a configuration file to NVRAM. **Answer B is correct; the `copy tftp flash` command erases the Flash RAM and loads a new IOS image from the TFTP server.** Answer C is incorrect; `copy tftp run` loads a new configuration into RAM. Answer D is incorrect; you cannot copy any file type to ROM.

7. If the last digit of the configuration register is 1, where will the router load the IOS from?

A. ROM

B. Flash

C. RAM

D. NVRAM

Answer A is correct; when the boot field (the last digit) is 1, the router is set to boot from ROM. Answer B is incorrect; the boot field would read 2 if Flash was to be booted from. Answer C is incorrect; IOS is not contained in the router's RAM. Answer D is incorrect; the IOS cannot be contained in NVRAM.

8. To check the name of the current IOS image, you would use the command (select all that apply):

A. `show run`

B. `show start`

C. `show ver`

D. `show flash`

Answer A is incorrect; `show run` does not supply the name of the current IOS image. Answer B is incorrect; it also does not provide information about the IOS image. **Answer C is correct; `show ver` provides the version of the IOS and the image file being used.** Answer D is incorrect; `show flash` shows all

IOS images held in Flash. So, only the show ver command really provides information on the currently loaded IOS, although if only one IOS image is present in Flash, you assume that it has been loaded on the router.

Cheat Sheet

The `boot host` configuration command can be used to load the startup-configuration from alternative locations, such as a TFTP server.

The `copy startup-config tftp` command is used at the privileged prompt to copy the startup configuration to a TFTP server.

The `copy running-config tftp` command can be used to copy your running configuration to a TFTP server.

The `copy tftp run` and `copy tftp start` commands enable you to copy a running or startup configuration from a TFTP server, respectively.

The `boot system` command can be used at the configuration prompt to specify where you want the IOS image to load from.

The `copy flash tftp` command enables you to back up your IOS image.

The `copy tftp flash` command enables you to load a new IOS image on the router.

The `show ver` command provides information on the currently running IOS image and shows the configuration registry for the router.

The `show flash` command enables you to view the current contents of the router's Flash RAM.

Network Protocols—TCP/IP

Cisco has divided its CCNA exam objectives into nine categories. Category 3 covers network protocols, Category 4 covers routing, and Category 5 covers WAN protocols. This chapter covers one of the objectives in the "Network Protocols" category—TCP/IP—and one of the objectives in the "Routing" category—ICMP (see the following list). This chapter also covers DNS, which falls under the "WAN Protocols" category (but would be more appropriately categorized under Network Management).

- TCP/IP
- ICMP
- DNS

TCP/IP

TCP/IP is the de facto network protocol for internetworking. This means that you must have a good handle on how IP addressing works (especially subnetting) and the protocols that make up the TCP/IP stack, particularly the protocols that reside at the Transport and Network layers of the OSI model. You also must know how to configure IP addresses, IP routing, and related routing protocols on a Cisco router.

IP addresses provide 32 bits of information (4 bytes). The addresses themselves are represented in a dotted decimal fashion in which the 32 bits are divided into 4 octets. An example of an IP address in dotted decimal is 130.1.16.1. You should understand that the dotted decimal format is used as a convenience, because the router actually sees the address as part of a bitstream—meaning a binary number.

The address 130.1.16.1 would be represented in binary as

10000010 00000001 00010000 00000001

IP addressing provides a hierarchical system that uniquely identifies devices on a network. Each address can tell you the network on which the device resides, the subnet to which it belongs (if subnetting has taken place), and the actual device address (also commonly referred to as the *host address* or the *node address*).

The Importance of Subnet Masks

Understanding which part of the IP address refers to the network, subnet, or device is a very important aspect of working with IP addresses. And you can't really tell this information without seeing the subnet mask that goes with the IP address.

Subnet masks are also typically represented as four dotted decimal octets. A standard subnet mask exists for each of the IP address classes (discussed in the next section). For example, the IP address 10.1.1.1 (a class A address) would have the standard Class A subnet mask of (remember there is no subnetting at this point) 255.0.0.0.

This combination of the IP address and subnet mask enables you to determine which portion of the address is the network address and which portion provides the host address (the router actually uses a process called *Anding* to determine the network address information for a particular IP address). Because the 255 (all ones in binary) "ands" out the network portion of the address, only the first octet of the address—10.1.1.1—specifies the network address (10.0.0.0). In addition, the second, third, and fourth octets provide the host addressing (0.1.1.1).

IP Address Classes

The designers of the IP addressing system saw IP addresses as falling into classes of addresses that were defined for networks of varying sizes. For example, very large networks would belong to a particular class (because of their need for many IP addresses), whereas small networks would belong to a different class (needing far fewer IP addresses). This type of addressing scheme is called *classful addressing*.

Three address classes are used for IP addressing:

- **Class A**—Used for very large networks. The default subnet mask is 255.0.0.0. Class A networks range from 1.0.0.0 through 126.0.0.0 and provide 16,777,214 host addresses. This is because the second, third, and fourth octets are available for host addressing. ARPAnet is an example of a Class A network. Class A addresses (that are not submitted) provide network and host information in the format network.host.host.host.

- **Class B**—Used for networks that still need many node addresses, such as a large company or institution. Class B ranges from 128.0.0.0 to 191.0.0.0. The default subnet mask is 255.255.0.0, and 16,384 Class B network addresses are available, with each Class B supplying 65,534 host addresses. The third and fourth octets are available for host addressing. Class B addresses provide network and host information in the format network.network.host.host.

- **Class C**—Used for small networks; 2,097,152 Class C networks exist. Class C addresses range from 192.0.0.0 to 223.0.0.0. The default subnet mask is 255.255.255.0. Class C networks provide 254 host addresses per network because only the fourth octet is reserved for host addressing. Class C address provide the network and host information in the format network.network.network.host.

Two other classes of addresses exist: Class D and Class E. Class D is used for IP multicasting, and Class E is reserved for research use. You don't need to worry about these two classes for the exam. Also, I should mention why 127.0.0.0 doesn't fall into any of the class ranges mentioned previously: It is reserved for loopback testing.

You must memorize the first octet range for each class so you can quickly identify the class of an IP address found on the exam. We've already discussed the fact that the router sees IP addresses in binary as it sifts through the bitstream. So, whereas you see an IP address such as 15.1.1.1 and know that it is a Class A address (because the first octet falls in between 1 and 126), the router sees the address as the following:

00001111 00000001 00000001 00000001

The router looks at the first octet and sees that the first bit is set to 0. The router immediately knows that this is a Class A address. This is known as the *first octet rule*. Table 6.1 summarizes the bit pattern the router uses to determine the class of a particular address.

Table 6.1 Bit Patterns Used by the Router

First Octet Lead Bits (Binary)	First Octet Range (Decimal)	Address Class
0	1–126	A
10	128–191	B
110	192–223	C

Memorize the first octet ranges for the classes and know the first octet rule and lead bits for each class. We will take a look at converting binary to decimal and vice versa in the subnetting section of this chapter.

TCP/IP, OSI, and DOD

The CCNA exam will pose several questions related to how protocols in the TCP/IP stack relate to the various layers of the OSI model, particularly the Transport and Network layers. Be aware, however, that when TCP/IP was developed in the 1970s, it preceded the completion of the OSI model (in the 1980s). So, the Department of Defense (DOD) developed its own conceptual model—the DOD model (also known as the DARPA model)—for how the various protocols in the TCP/IP stack operate. This reference model divides the movement of data from a sending node to a receiving node into four layers (compared to the seven layers of the OSI model). The following figure shows the comparative mappings of the OSI model, DOD model, and TCP/IP stack.

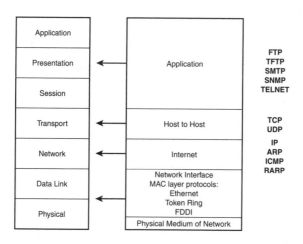

Because we've already taken a look at the OSI model (in Chapter 1, "The OSI Reference Model"), a short description of the DOD model layers and some of the TCP/IP protocols (those that are important for the CCNA exam) that operate at those layers is provided. This figure provides a mapping of the OSI model to the DOD model and to the TCP/IP stack.

The Application layer protocols provide the user interface for the various protocols/applications that access the network. Application layer protocols in the TCP/IP stack handle file transfer, remote login to other nodes, email functionality, and network monitoring.

Each of the TCP/IP Application layer protocols is assigned a well-known port number (as are other TCP/IP stack members that work at other layers, such as TCP and UDP). The port number is used by Transport layer protocols to identify the upper-layer protocol that is sending or receiving data (more about ports and sockets in the next section). You should be familiar with the following Application layer protocols (you might as well memorize their port numbers, as well):

- **FTP (File Transfer Protocol)**—A protocol that provides the capability to transfer files between two computers. FTP is actually a full-blown application and provides the capability to list files to be downloaded. FTP uses port 21.

- **TFTP (Trivial File Transfer Protocol)**—A stripped-down version of FTP that provides a way to move files without any type of authentication (meaning no username and password) or the capability to list the files available. TFTP uses port 69.

- **Telnet**—A terminal emulation protocol that enables you to connect a local computer with a remote computer (or other device, such as a router). The local computer becomes a virtual terminal that has access to applications and other resources on the remote computer. Telnet uses port 23. (Telnet is discussed in more detail in Chapter 3, "The Cisco IOS—Basic Router Commands.")

- **SMTP (Simple Mail Transport Protocol)**—A protocol that provides mail delivery between two computers. It is a protocol supported by email clients used for sending and receiving email on the Internet. SMTP uses port 25.

- **SNMP (Simple Network Management Protocol)**—A protocol that provides the capability to collect network information. SNMP uses agents that collect data on network performance. SNMP uses port 169.

- **DNS (Domain Name System)**—A protocol that translates names of network nodes into IP addresses. DNS uses UDP on port 53.

Other protocols, such as DNS, HTTP, and so on, also function at the Application layer of the DOD model. Be sure you are familiar with Telnet and TFTP for the exam.

TCP/IP Transport Layer

For the CCNA exam, you must know the two different strategies for the movement of packets at the Transport layer of the TCP/IP stack. (Also, remember that the OSI Transport layer is equivalent to the Host-to-Host layer on the DOD model.) The two methods are *connection-oriented* and *connectionless-oriented* transport as handled by the Transport Control Protocol (TCP) and the User Datagram Protocol (UDP), respectively. We talked in very general terms about connection-oriented versus connectionless transport in Chapter 2, "Layered Communication and Connectivity."

TCP is a connection-oriented transport protocol operating on port 6. TCP provides transport services for upper-layer protocols (protocols in the Application layer of the DOD model). These protocols supply TCP with the data, a destination address, and the port number that identifies the application—for example, FTP is port 21.

The destination IP address and port number provide TCP with a socket, which is used on both the sending and receiving computers as the connection points for the data transfer. This use of port numbers along with destination IP addresses (forming a socket) enables sending and receiving computers to distinguish different data streams between upper-layer applications.

Three things that you should definitely remember about TCP for the exam relate to how TCP establishes a connection with the destination host, how reliable data transfer is accomplished, and the flow control mechanisms embraced by TCP:

- **TCP Connection**—TCP uses a three-way handshake method of establishing the connection between the sending and receiving host. The sending computer will initiate the connection with a synchronization and connection request. The receiving computer then acknowledges the request and requests a TCP connection. The sending computer acknowledges the request from the receiving computer, and then initiates the transfer of data.

- **Reliable Data Transfer**—TCP provides reliable data transfer by creating a dedicated path across the network for the packets. All packets move along this static path sequentially. When the established connection is no longer needed, the connection is terminated.

- **Flow Control Mechanisms**—TCP uses a system of acknowledgements between the sending and receiving computers to control the data flow. TCP embraces flow control mechanisms, such as windowing and source-quench messages, to protect the buffer on the receiving computer (flow control is discussed in Chapter 2).

UDP provides connectionless communication at the Transport layer of the TCP/IP stack. UDP is on port 17 and provides best effort transport of data across the network. UDP does not use acknowledgements or flow control mechanisms. This means that UDP requires less overhead.

The paths for packets are selected on a packet-by-packet basis, and bandwidth is also dynamically allocated on an as-needed basis. UDP uses sockets for the communication of upper-layer protocols on the sending and receiving computers as does TCP. The thing to remember about UDP is that it doesn't embrace any of the connection handshake, flow control, or sequencing strategies you see in TCP.

TCP/IP Network Layer

The main function of the Network layer is the addressing of packets for delivery and their routing across the internetwork. The OSI Network layer maps to the DOD Internet layer. As far as the TCP/IP stack is concerned, you should be particularly familiar with these protocols: IP, ARP, RARP, and ICMP (ICMP is covered in the next objective).

- **IP (Internet Protocol)**—IP takes the data from the Transport layer and fragments the information into packets or datagrams. IP also labels each packet with the IP address of the sending device and the IP address of the receiving device. In addition, IP reassembles datagrams on the receiving machine into segments for the upper-layer protocols. IP is a connectionless protocol that has no interest in the contents of the datagrams. Its only desire is to address and move the datagrams toward their final destination.

- **ARP (Address Resolution Protocol)**—When IP prepares a datagram, it knows the IP address of the sending and receiving computers (it receives this information from the upper-layer protocols, such as Telnet or SMTP). IP also requires the MAC hardware address for the receiving computer because it must provide this information to the Network Access layer protocol used on the network (such as Ethernet). ARP provides the mechanism for resolving the IP address to an actual hardware address.

- **RARP (Reverse Address Resolution Protocol)**—RARP does the opposite of ARP and resolves IP addresses to MAC addresses. It is typically used by diskless workstations because a diskless workstation will not have an IP address upon bootup and must acquire one to join the network.

For the exam, you really need to know the ins and outs of IP addressing, including subnetting, which is discussed later in this chapter. As far as the other Network layer protocols go, know the difference between ARP and RARP. A little more information is also warranted on ARP in relation to routed data.

When a computer wants to send data to a computer that resides on the same subnet, the sending computer uses an ARP broadcast to resolve the IP address of the receiving computer to that computer's MAC hardware address. The receiving computer responds to the broadcast and lets the sending computer know its MAC address.

In cases where the receiving computer is on a different subnet, the router (the default gateway for the sending computer) becomes involved in the process. The router actually responds to the ARP broadcast from the sending computer and supplies the MAC address of its LAN interface. The packets are then sent to the router interface, and the router then uses its routing table to determine the next hop for the packets.

Other protocols in the TCP/IP stack operate at the Network layer, such as RIP and IGRP. We discuss these protocols in Chapter 8, "Internetwork Routing."

IP Addresses and Subnetting

You definitely need to know the various classes of IP address first octet ranges (A, B, and C) discussed at the beginning of this chapter and the default subnet mask for each class. You also must be able to determine the new subnet mask for a particular class network address that has been subnetted and be able to determine the valid ranges of IP addresses available for the subnet you create.

The subnetting of IP networks is accomplished by taking bits that are normally used for host addressing and using these bits to create subnets. Two approaches exist for successfully answering the IP subnet questions on the CCNA exam: You can memorize the charts that follow for Class A, B, and C networks or you can learn to do the math (explained in a moment).

Without being able to do the math, however, the charts can fail you if subnetting on more than one octet is required for the exam question. So, first the charts: Tables 6.2, 6.3, and 6.4 show you the number of bits borrowed (from one octet only), the new subnet mask that would result, the number of subnets that would become available, and the number of host addresses that would be available (after subnetting) for a Class A, Class B, and Class C network, respectively.

Table 6.2 Class A Subnetting

Bits Used	Subnet Mask	# Of Subnets	Hosts/Subnet
2	255.192.0.0	2	4,194,302
3	255.224.0.0	6	2,097,150
4	255.240.0.0	14	1,048,574
5	255.248.0.0	30	524,286
6	255.252.0.0	62	262,142
7	255.254.0.0	126	131,070
8	255.255.0.0	254	65,534

Table 6.3 Class B Subnetting

Bits Used	Subnet Mask	# of Subnets	Hosts/Subnet
2	255.255.192.0	2	16,382
3	255.255.224.0	6	8,190
4	255.255.240.0	14	4,094
5	255.255.248.0	30	2,046
6	255.255.252.0	62	1,022
7	255.255.254.0	126	510
8	255.255.255.0	254	254

Table 6.4 Class C Subnetting

Bits Used	Subnet Mask	# of Subnets	Hosts/Subnet
2	255.255.255.192	2	62
3	255.255.255.224	6	30
4	255.255.255.240	14	14
5	255.255.255.248	30	6
6	255.255.255.252	62	2

If you can memorize these tables and write them down on the scratch paper they provide you for the exam, you will be in very good shape to answer IP subnetting questions. Here are a couple of tricks for building a chart from the bottom up, if you find that you can't memorize the whole chart (or panic just before you begin the exam). All you have to do is remember the last entry.

For example, if you are working with a Class A network, a fully subnetted second octet (all 8 bits used) yields 254 subnets with 65,534 addresses available per subnet. You know that the next step up in the chart would use 7 bits for subnetting.

To get the number of subnets that would be available, take the 254 from the last entry in the chart, divide it by 2, and subtract 1 (254/2–1=126). So, 126 is the number of subnets yielded by borrowing 7 bits.

To figure out the number of host addresses that would be available per subnet when you have 7 bits borrowed, take the number from the 8-bit results (65,534), double it, and then add 2 (65,534×2+2=131,070). Therefore, 131,070 is the hosts/subnet.

Remember that you have time before you start the test to write things down on your scratch sheet or that little white board that is provided (you might want to ask the exam provider to give you some extra sheets just to be safe). So, make sure that you either write down the charts or get ready to do the math as discussed in the sections that follow.

Converting Decimal to Binary

When you subnet a network, you must determine the number of bits that will be used for your subnets. Host bits are then used to create the subnets. This means that you reduce the number of host addresses that are available for your network. This borrowing or stealing of bits is typically done by borrowing bits from the first available octet of the network address. For example, on a Class A network of 11.0.0.0, the bits that would be used for subnetting would come from the second octet.

Before we get into issues related to planning the subnets so that the appropriate number of IP addresses (the actual number of host addresses needed for your computers) are available on each subnet, you must know how to convert decimal information to binary and vice versa.

Each octet consists of eight bits, which are represented by a decimal number. Each bit in the octet carries a different decimal value when it is actually turned on (set to 1). From left to right, the bits have the following decimal values:

128 64 32 16 8 4 2 1

So, an octet with the decimal value of 96 would be converted to binary as follows:

0 1 1 0 0 0 0 0

Because the decimal value is less than 128, the first bit is set to 0. The second bit value of 64 is less than our octet decimal value of 96, so that bit is set to 1. Now take 96–64=32. This means you will set the third bit to 1 because it carries a value of 32. Now, because 64+32=96, all the other bits are set to 0; they have no value.

Approaching conversions in the opposite direction (from binary to decimal), let's say you have the binary values for an octet as follows:

1 0 0 1 0 0 1 0

The first bit is set to 1, so you have 128. The fourth bit is set to 1, resulting in 16. The seventh bit is set to 1, which equals 2. Then, you add them together: 128+16+2=146. The decimal value of the octet is 146. When you work with an octet in binary, the bits on the left side of the octet are referred to as the higher-order bits. The bits on the right side of the octet are referred to as the lower-order bits.

Computing Subnet Masks

Now let's take a look at computing the new subnet mask for a network that has been subnetted. I've seen the math for computing subnet masks, subnet ranges, and number of host addresses done in a bunch of different ways. I'm going to provide you with what I think is the simplest and fastest way to find these values when you are working on the exam.

In the real world, you would plan your network carefully, estimating how many host addresses will be needed at each corporate location (meaning on each subnet, with the plan including some room for growth); you would then figure out the number of subnets—and this is how Cisco will craft its exam questions. We will go over this several times in the practice exam. But, for now, let's keep our example simple and look at a case in which we know the number of subnets we want to create.

For example, suppose you have the Class B network address of 180.10.0.0. The first two octets provide network information and so are not available for subnetting. This means that the first available octet you can steal bits from for subnetting is the third octet. You want to create 14 subnets. Here's how you do the math.

First, write down the decimal equivalents for a binary octet:

128 64 32 16 8 4 2 1

You want 14 subnets. The formula you use is (sum of lower-order bits)–1. You cannot use subnet 0, which is what you derive when you steal only the first lower-order bit (that is why you must subtract 1 from the total). So, you add the 1, 2, 4, and 8 bits: 1+2+4+8=15. Subtract 1, and you get 14. Therefore, to create 14 subnets, you must borrow 4 lower-order bits.

Now, you know how many bits are needed to create the 14 subnets. To create the new subnet mask (remember, you are computing the new decimal number that will appear in the third position of the subnet mask), you add the first 4 higher-order bits: 128+64+32+16=240.

The default subnet mask for Class B networks is 255.255.0.0. Therefore, the new subnet mask for your network that will be divided into 14 subnets is 255.255.240.0.

This procedure will work for all three classes of IP addresses. All you have to do is place the correct computed mask number in the appropriate octet.

Calculating Host Addresses Available

Computing the number of host addresses available per subnet is very straightforward. The formula you use is 2^X-2; where X is the number of bits left for host addresses after bits have been borrowed for subnetting.

For example, in a Class A network that has not been subnetted, 24 bits (3 octets) are available for host addresses. If you subnet the Class A network into 62 subnets, you must borrow 6 bits. The lower-order bits borrowed would be 1, 2, 4, 8, 16, and 32; add them (1+2+4+8+16+32=63) and then subtract 1, and you get 62. This means that the 6 bits are unavailable for host addresses. Therefore, you take the total host bits normally available (24), subtract 6 from it, and you get 18 (24–6=18).

Now you can use the 2^X-2 formula, where $2^{18}-2=262,142$. This results in 262,142 host addresses being available per subnet.

Calculating Subnet Address Ranges

You also must be able to calculate the range of addresses that are valid for each subnet on your network. Let's walk through the subnetting of a Class A network and also look at a quick way to determine the valid address ranges for the subnets.

Say your network is a Class A 10.0.0.0 and you want to create 30 subnets. You must steal 5 lower-order bits to create the 30 subnets: (1+2+4+8+16)–1=30. Then you take the first 5 higher-order bits and add them (128+64+32+16+8=248). The network subnet mask therefore is 255.248.0.0.

The number of host addresses per subnet would be 2^X-2, where X is 24–5=19. So, $2^{19}-2=524,286$. Now, let's look at how you get the ranges of IP addresses for each subnet.

The lowest higher-order bit that was used to create the new subnet mask was 8; so 8 becomes the increment for your subnets. You use the increment as the step for each subnet range.

The first available address for subnet 1 (of 30) is 10.8.0.1, where the increment of 8 is placed in the second octet position. The first available address for subnet 2 is quickly computed by adding 8 to the second octet: 10.16.0.1.

Now, before we figure out the ending address for each of these subnets, we need to look at why 10.8.0.0 and 10.16.0.0 are not valid addresses for these two subnets, respectively. These addresses serve as the subnet addresses, or as Cisco calls them, the network addresses. They designate the subnet (10.0.0.0 would be called the *major* network address). They cannot be assigned to hosts.

To figure out the ending address for the subnet range, you subtract 1 from the beginning address of the next subnet. For example, to find the ending address for 10.8.0.0, you subtract 1 from 16 and get 15. So, the range beginning with 10.8.0.1 will end with 10.15.255.254.

A very good reason exists why you can't end the range with 10.15.255.255. It is the broadcast address for the subnet. If you converted the address 10.15.255.255 to binary you would find that all the host bits are set to 1s, which is the way that broadcast messages are addressed to all nodes on the subnet.

Table 6.5 gives the start and end addresses for the first 10 of the 30 subnets that would be created from the major network 10.0.0.0. To figure out the other 20 ranges, simply add the increment (8) to the second octet (the subnet octet). Remember that each range will have a network address and a broadcast address that cannot be used for addressing hosts.

Table 6.5   IP Address Ranges for Subnets (First 10 of 30)

Subnet #	Start Address	End Address
1	10.8.0.1	10.15.255.254
2	10.16.0.1	10.23.255.254
3	10.24.0.1	10.31.255.254
4	10.32.0.1	10.39.255.254
5	10.40.0.1	10.47.255.254
6	10.48.0.1	10.55.255.254
7	10.56.0.1	10.63.255.254
8	10.64.0.1	10.71.255.254
9	10.72.0.1	10.79.255.254
10	10.80.0.1	10.87.255.254

Determining the valid range of subnet addresses, the network address, and the broadcast address for Class C networks is not quite as intuitive as Class A and Class B networks. For example, let's say that you have the Class C major network address of 220.1.1.0. To divide the network into 2 subnets, you must steal 2 bits from the fourth octet. This creates the network subnet mask of 255.255.255.192.

Because you stole 2 bits for the subnets, 6 bits are left for host addresses: $2^6-2=62$. So, you end up with 62 host addresses per subnet. Taking the lowest of the higher-order bits used to create the network subnet mask, which is 64, you can create the range of addresses for the two subnets.

For the first subnet range, the first address—220.1.1.64—is the network address for the subnet (you can't use it for a host address). The first address of the next subnet range and the network address for the second subnet is 220.1.1.128.

This means the range of valid host addresses for the first subnet is 220.1.1.65–220.1.1.126. The address 220.1.1.127 (one address before the beginning of the second subnet range) has all the host bits set to 1 (when the address is converted to binary), so this address is the broadcast address for the subnet.

For the second subnet, the valid host address range would be 220.1.1.129–220.1.1.190, with the last address in the range (220.1.1.191) being the broadcast address for the subnet.

Router Subnet Mask Notation

When you work on the router, you will find that the Cisco IOS has its own notation for specifying subnet masks and for entering the subnet mask during the initial configuration dialog (entered using the setup command). The following figure shows the results of the show interface Ethernet 0 command. Notice that the IP address for the interface is 10.3.1.1. The subnet mask is specified by the /16. This means that the entire 8 bits from the second octet were used for the subnetting of this Class A network (8 network bits + 8 subnet bits). This would make the subnet mask 255.255.0.0 (because you used all 8 bits in the second octet, add all the decimal values of the bits: 128+64+32+16+8+4+2+1=255).

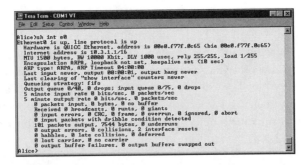

When you configure IP addresses for router interfaces using the Setup dialog, you must provide the subnet mask for the interface by entering the number of bits that have been borrowed for subnetting. The next figure shows the settings for an Ethernet interface in which a Class A network has been subnetted into 14 subnets. The Setup dialog asks for the number of bits in the subnet field. This is the number of bits borrowed for subnets and in this case would be 4.

```
Tera Term - COM1 VT
File Edit Setup Control Window Help
The enable secret is a one-way cryptographic secret used
instead of the enable password when it exists.

    Enter enable secret: password

The enable password is used when there is no enable secret
and when using older software and some boot images.

    Enter enable password: cisco
    Enter virtual terminal password: password
    Configure SNMP Network Management? [yes]: no
    Configure DECnet? [no]:
    Configure AppleTalk? [no]:
    Configure IPX? [no]:
    Configure IP? [yes]:
        Configure IGRP routing? [yes]: no
        Configure RIP routing? [no]:
    Configure bridging? [no]:

Configuring interface parameters:

Configuring interface Ethernet0:
    Is this interface in use? [yes]:
    Configure IP on this interface? [yes]:
        IP address for this interface: 10.16.1.1
        Number of bits in subnet field [0]: 4
        Class A network is 10.0.0.0, 4 subnet bits; mask is /12
    Enable all hub ports on this interface? [yes]:

Configuring interface Serial0:
    Is this interface in use? [yes]:
    Configure IP on this interface? [yes]:
    Configure IP unnumbered on this interface? [no]:
        IP address for this interface: 10.32.1.1
        Number of bits in subnet field [4]:
        Class A network is 10.0.0.0, 4 subnet bits; mask is /12

Configuring interface Serial1:
    Is this interface in use? [yes]:
    Configure IP on this interface? [yes]:
    Configure IP unnumbered on this interface? [no]:
        IP address for this interface: 10.48.1.1
```

Configuring IP Addresses

IP addresses are assigned to interfaces on the router in the interface configuration mode. The configuration command is ip address followed by the IP address of the interface and the subnet mask for the interface.

Remember that, if you are connecting two routers over a LAN or WAN connection, the connection constitutes one subnet. This means that the router interfaces must be configured with IP addresses from the same subnet.

The following figure shows the configuration of an Ethernet interface and a Serial interface on a router. This router has been configured as part of a Class A network that has been divided into 254 subnets.

```
Tera Term - COM1 VT
File Edit Setup Control Window Help
Alice(config)#int e0
Alice(config-if)#ip address 10.3.1.1 255.255.0.0
Alice(config-if)#no shut
Alice(config-if)#int s0
Alice(config-if)#ip address 10.2.1.2 255.255.0.0
Alice(config-if)#no shut
Alice(config-if)#
```

The no shut commands that are placed after the IP address command are used to "bounce" the router interface into the up mode. This helps ensure that the interface is active. After completing the IP address configuration of an interface or interfaces, Ctrl+Z or End can be used to end the configuration session and return to the privileged prompt.

115

15

ICMP

ICMP (Internet Control Message Protocol) is a messaging service and management protocol for IP. ICMP plays several different roles in the routing process and is therefore considered an important exam objective by Cisco. ICMP messages are actually carried as IP datagrams. ICMP plays some important roles related to routing, and ICMP messages are also used by ping and traceroute (discussed in the "ping and traceroute" section at the end of this chapter).

ICMP Messages

ICMP provides several different messages that are used by the routers to communicate with host computers on the network and to verify a particular connection. Table 6.6 provides a list of the ICMP message types you should know for the CCNA exam.

Table 6.6   ICMP Message Types

Message Type	Used For
Destination Unreachable	Lets a host computer know that the router cannot forward an IP packet any further.
Time to Live Exceeded	Lets a host computer know that the packet's time to live has been exceeded. The router can't send the packet on to the next hop (the router is called the executioner router because it "kills" the packet), so the packet has been discarded. The traceroute command uses TTL exceeded messages to trace the route to a particular IP address.

Table 6.6 continued

Message Type	Used For
Buffer Full (source quench)	If the router's buffer is full, a source-quench message is sent out to the source host.
Redirect	If a router receives packets from a host that should have been sent to a router that provides a better router, an ICMP packet is sent to the host telling it to use the other router.
Echo	Used by ping to determine the viability of a particular IP address on the inter-network.

In a nutshell, ICMP is mainly available as a way for host computers to acquire router information on the internetwork. In fact, ICMP provides the message types used by two IOS commands, ping and traceroute, that are used to test IP connections and verify IP addresses.

ping **and** traceroute

Two Cisco IOS commands are used to test IP connectivity and verify IP addresses on router interfaces or hosts on your internetwork: ping and traceroute (a third command, telnet, can also be used to test Application layer connectivity and is discussed in Chapter 3).

ping provides a quick way to test the connection between two nodes on the internetwork. *Ping* stands for Packet Internet Gopher and uses ICMP echo packets to test the connection. The command syntax is ping *ip address*, where *ip address* is the IP address of the target device (this can be another router's interface, a host computer, or other network device). The following figure shows the ping command being used to test the connection between two routers.

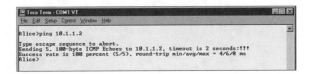

The trace command (or traceroute) enables you to see the route the packets take from source to destination. As already mentioned, traceroute uses TTL exceeded messages to trace the route to a particular IP address. This command actually enables you to see how packets are being routed across the internetwork. The command syntax is trace *ip address*. The following figure shows that the packets moved across one router interface (10.2.1.1) to get to the destination IP address of 10.1.1.2.

Both ping and trace can be used to troubleshoot IP connectivity. More about troubleshooting routed environments is discussed in Chapter 11, "Access Lists and Network Troubleshooting."

16

DNS

Because most routed environments are TCP/IP environments, you must understand how DNS (domain name system) is involved in name resolution. For the exam, you should know what DNS is and its importance on routed networks.

The DNS provides a hierarchical name resolution strategy for resolving a fully qualified domain name (FQDN) to an IP address. DNS servers provide this "friendly name"-to-logical address (the IP address) resolution (and vice versa) on TCP/IP networks.

DNS and the Internet

On the Internet (an extremely large TCP/IP network), each organization (a company, institution, or other entity) will deploy DNS servers that provide FQDN resolution to IP addresses for its organization. In effect, each large company, organization, or service provider manages the name resolution duties for its own portion of the Internet. In fact, when a company registers a domain name with InterNIC, the IP addresses of two DNS servers must be provided that will handle the name resolution duties for that domain.

At the base of the DNS tree is the *root* domain. The Internet's root domain is represented by a period (see the following figure). Below the root domain on the inverted DNS tree are the *top-level* domains. The top-level domains consist of the suffixes .com, .edu, .gov, and so on.

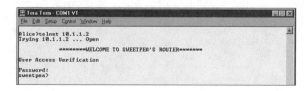

Below the top-level domains are the *second-level* domains. These secondary domains consist of company, institutional, and private domains that we commonly use to access a Web site, such as macmillanusa.com (Macmillan USA's domain name) and american.edu (the domain name of the American University in Washington, D.C.). Under the second-level domains are *subdomains*, which are typically used to divide a larger secondary domain into geographical or functional units. This inverted tree structure is referred to as the DNS *namespace*.

DNS Zones

Although the DNS hierarchy provides for domains at various levels, the DNS namespace can be further divided into *zones*. A zone is a discrete part of the domain namespace that can be used to create management segments in a domain; a different administrator could manage each zone.

Zones really become partitions in the domain namespace. Each zone has a DNS nameserver, which holds the zone database for that zone. This zone database provides the entire hostname to IP address mappings for the computers and other devices in that zone. Zones would typically be linked by routers and be subsets of a particular company's or institution's total LAN/WAN implementation.

Two zone categories exist: forward lookup zones and reverse lookup zones. A forward lookup zone allows for forward lookup queries, which enables a host to find the IP address using the hostname of a particular computer or device. For DNS to work, at least one forward lookup zone is required. A reverse lookup zone allows for the resolving of IP addresses to hostnames, which is called a reverse lookup query.

Because DNS enables unicast communication on the network between hosts and DNS servers (rather than using broadcast messages for name resolution, which would not be forwarded by a router), DNS requests can be routed over a network by routers. This is why several DNS servers are deployed on a large network to avoid overtaxing routers with name resolution requests from nodes on the network.

TAKE THE TEST

This Practice Test provides you with questions related to objectives in three different CCNA exam categories: the "Network Protocols" category's TCP/IP objective, the "Routing" category's ICMP objective, and the "WAN Protocols" category's DNS objective. Because the CCNA exam is in a multiple-choice format, these questions are formatted as they would be on the actual exam.

1. What is the network number for a node with the IP address 130.1.1.1?

   A. 130.0.0.0

   B. 130.1.0.0

   C. 255.255.0.0

   D. 0.0.1.1

Answer A is incorrect; this address is a Class B address, meaning the network ID is contained in the first two octets. **Answer B is correct; the network ID for a Class B address is the first two octets.** Answer C is incorrect; this is the default subnet mask for a Class B network. Answer D is incorrect; the last two octets of a Class B address provide node information (when the network is not subnetted).

2. The first octet decimal range for Class C networks is

   A. 1–126

   B. 192–223

   C. 128–191

   D. 127

Answer A is incorrect; this is the first octet range for Class A networks. **Answer B is correct; this is the range for Class C networks.** Answer C is incorrect; this is the range for Class B networks. Answer D is incorrect; this first octet number is reserved for the loopback function.

3. The DOD model from the top of the stack down contains the following layers:

    A. Application, Presentation, Session, Transport, Network, Data Link, and Physical

    B. Telnet, TCP, and IP

    C. Network Interface, Internet, Host to Host, and Application

    D. Application, Host to Host, Internet, and Network Interface

Answer A is incorrect; it lists the layers of the OSI model. Answer B is incorrect; it lists protocols in the TCP/IP stack. Answer C is incorrect; it lists the layers of the DOD model from the bottom up. **Answer D is correct; it shows the layers of the DOD model from the top down.**

4. Which of the following is a Transport layer, connection-oriented protocol in the TCP/IP stack?

    A. UDP

    B. Telnet

    C. TCP

    D. IP

Answer A is incorrect; UDP is a connectionless protocol operating at the Transport layer. Answer B is incorrect; Telnet is an Application layer protocol. **Answer C is correct; TCP is a Transport layer, connection-oriented protocol.** Answer D is incorrect; IP is a Network layer protocol (and connectionless).

5. Which TCP/IP stack protocol is used for source-quench messages from routers to host computers?

    A. UDP

    B. IP

    C. ARP

    D. ICMP

Answer A is incorrect; UDP provides connectionless transport. Answer B is incorrect; IP provides logical addressing. Answer C is incorrect; ARP provides

IP address-to-MAC address resolution. **Answer D is correct; ICMP packets are used for source-quench messages.**

6. You have been assigned a Class B network address of 132.1.0.0. You need to subnet your network to conserve network bandwidth. You need more than 1,000 host addresses at each site, and projected need puts the host address account eventually at 1,500 for each subnet. You also want to create the greatest number of subnets that will still support the necessary host addresses. Calculate the maximum number of subnets that you can create and the subnet mask for the network:

  A. 62, 255.255.252.0

  B. 30, 255.248.0.0

  C. 30, 255.255.248.0

  D. 14, 255.255.240.0

Answer A is incorrect; a Class B network divided into 62 subnets provides only 1,022 host addresses/subnets, which will not support the expected growth. Answer B is incorrect; the subnet mask provided is for a Class A network divided into 30 subnets. **Answer C is correct; 30 subnets provide 2,046 host addresses, and the subnet mask is correctly configured for a Class B network with 30 subnets. To get the correct answer, you could refer to the Class B subnetting chart you've memorized and written down for the test. Or, you could begin to steal bits from the third octet and use the formula 2^x-2 to find the maximum number of bits that could be stolen and still provide at least 1,500 IP addresses per subnet. Stealing 3 bits (16 total host bits minus 3) makes the formula $2^{13}-2=8$. This equals 190, which is not maximizing the subnets. Jump up to 5 bits: $2^{11}-2=2,046$. Add the 5 lower-order bits and you get 30 subnets. Take the first 5 higher-order bits and you get the subnet mask 255.255.248.0.** Answer D is incorrect; 14 subnets on a Class B network supplies 4,094 hosts but does not maximize the possible number of subnets (only supplying 14).

7. If the IP address 13.1.1.1 is accompanied by the subnet mask 255.255.0.0, how many subnets have been created on this network?

  A. 0

  B. 254

  C. 14

  D. 2

Answer A is incorrect; the IP address is a Class A address, not a Class B address; the subnet mask 255.255.0.0 on a Class B address would mean there are 0 subnets. **Answer B is correct; the IP address is a Class A address, and all the bits in the second octet have been used for subnetting; all 8 bits added with 1 bit subtracted for subnet 0 equals 254.** Answer C is incorrect; a Class A network with 14 subnets would have the subnet mask of 255.240.0.0. Answer D is incorrect; a Class A network with 2 subnets would have the subnet mask of 255.192.0.0.

8. If you used the show interface command and saw the information 135.1.2.1/23, what would the subnet mask for the interface be?

   A. 255.255.0.0

   B. 255.255.254.0

   C. 255.254.0

   D. 255.255.252.0

Answer A is incorrect; this is a Class B address, and the mask parameter would be /16 for a Class B network with no subnetting, which would translate to 255.255.0.0. **Answer B is correct; 23–16 (the normal network bits for a Class B)=7. Then, if you add the first 7 higher-order bits, you get 254, making 255.255.254.0 the correct subnet mask.** Answer C is incorrect; this is a mask for a subnetted Class A network. Answer D is incorrect; 252 would be equivalent to /22: the 16 bits plus 6 for subnetting.

9. Which of the following commands executed on the router would correctly configure an interface with an IP address?

   A. `router<config> ip address 10.3.1.1 255.255.0.0`

   B. `router<config-if> ip address 11.32.1.1 255.224.0.0`

   C. `router<config-if> ip address 220.1.1.1 255.0.0.0`

   D. `router# ip address 11.32.1.1 255.224.0.0`

Answer A is incorrect; you must be in the interface configuration mode to input an IP address. **Answer B is correct; the command is executed at the correct prompt and the Class A IP is accompanied by a valid Class A subnet mask.** Answer C is incorrect; a Class C address cannot be assigned a Class A subnet mask. Answer D is incorrect; you cannot configure a router interface at the privileged prompt.

10. Which IP address verification command provides the route to the destination address?

A. ping

B. telnet

C. ip address

D. trace

Answer A is incorrect; ping only verifies the connection to the destination address. Answer B is incorrect; telnet provides a terminal connection to a remote device. Answer C is incorrect; this is the command that is used to configure interfaces with IP addresses. **Answer D is correct; trace provides the route from the sending device to the receiving device.**

11. You are implementing a TCP/IP network. Which of these services would supply hostname-to-IP address resolution on your network?

A. ping

B. DHCP

C. DNS

D. traceroute

Answer A is incorrect; ping is used to test the viability of a particular IP address on the network. Answer B is incorrect; DHCP is used to assign IP addresses to network devices. **Answer C is correct; DNS provides hostname-to-IP address resolution.** Answer D is incorrect; traceroute is used to trace packets from a source address on the network to a destination IP address.

Cheat Sheet

Each IP address class provides network and node information:

Class A: network.node.node.node
Class B: network.network.node.node
Class C: network.network.network.node

Be sure you know the first octet range and default subnet mask for each of the IP address classes:

Class	First Octet Range	Number of Networks	Number of Hosts	Default Subnet Mask
A	1–126	127	16,777,214	255.0.0.0
B	128–191	16,384	65,534	255.255.0.0
C	192–223	2,097,152	254	255.255.255.0

FTP, Telnet, SMTP, SNMP, and TFTP are Application layer TCP/IP protocols.

TCP is a connection-oriented, Transport layer protocol that provides transport of packets over a defined network path and takes advantage of flow control mechanisms.

UDP is a connectionless, Transport layer protocol that provides best effort transport of data on a packet-by-packet basis.

IP is a connectionless, Network layer protocol that enables the logical addressing of packets.

ARP is a Network layer protocol that is used to resolve IP addresses to MAC addresses.

RARP is a Network layer protocol that is used to resolve MAC addresses to IP addresses (typically by diskless workstations).

IP protocols and port numbers:

Protocol	Port Number
TCP	6
UDP	17

Protocol	Port Number
FTP	21
Telnet	23
DNS	53
TFTP	69
SMTP	25
SNMP	162

Convert the decimal values of IP octets to binary or vice versa using the bit values 128, 64, 32, 16, 8, 4, 2, and 1.

To find the number of bits necessary to create a certain number of subnets, use the formula (sum of lower order bits)–1.

To create the subnet mask for a subnetted network, add the number of higher-order bits to the number of bits you stole to create the subnets.

To figure out the number of host addresses per subnet, use the formula 2^X-2, where X is the number of bits still available for host addressing (you must subtract the number of bits you stole for subnetting from the total number of host bits normally available for that network class).

IP addresses are configured for interfaces at the interface configuration prompt. The command is `ip address` followed by the IP address for the interface and the appropriate subnet mask.

The `ping` command is used to test the connection between two nodes on the network (the syntax is `ping` followed by the IP address of the destination).

The `traceroute` command provides the route between the sending device and the destination device (the syntax is `trace` followed by the destination IP address).

ICMP packets are used by routers to send messages to host machines. These include destination unreachable message, source-quench messages, time to live messages, and echo messages (used by `ping`).

Continued

DNS is the primary hostname-to-IP addressing service used on IP networks.

The DNS namespace takes the form of an inverted tree. At the top of the tree is the root domain.

The DNS namespace is partitioned into zones. Each zone has a database that provides the mappings for computer and other devices in that zone.

Two zone categories exist: forward lookup zones and reverse lookup zones. A *forward lookup zone* allows for forward lookup queries, which enable a host to find the IP address using the hostname of a particular computer or device. For DNS to work, at least one forward lookup zone is required. A *reverse lookup zone* enables the resolving of IP addresses to hostnames.

Network Protocols—IPX/SPX

Cisco has divided its CCNA exam objectives into nine categories. Category three covers network protocols. This chapter covers two of the objectives listed under the "Network Protocols" category (see the following list).

- Novell IPX
- IPX

17

Novell IPX

Novell NetWare is a popular network operating system (NOS) that has provided file and print server functionality to LANs since the early 1980s. NetWare has its own proprietary network protocol stack called IPX/SPX. IPX is similar to TCP/IP in that the protocols that make up the IPX/SPX stack do not directly map to the layers of the OSI model. IPX/SPX gained a strong foothold in early local area networking because IPX/SPX was strong on performance and did not require the overhead necessary to run TCP/IP.

For the exam, you should be aware of the different protocols that make up the IPX/SPX stack. For example, the *NetWare Core Protocol* (NCP) handles network functions at the Application, Presentation, and Session layers of the OSI model. The NetWare *VLMs (Virtual Loadable Modules)* establish and maintain network sessions between the client and server. More important to our discussion of routing are the IPX/SPX protocols that are involved in the routing process (see the following figure):

- **SPX (Sequence Packet Exchange)**—A connection-oriented transport protocol that provides the upper-layer protocols with a direct connection between the sending and receiving machines. SPX uses virtual circuits to provide the connection between computers and will display a connection ID in the SPX datagram header (SPX is similar to TCP in the TCP/IP protocol).

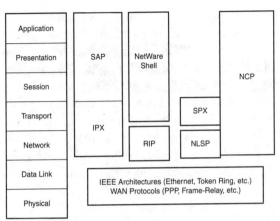

- **IPX (Internet Package Exchange Program)**—A connectionless transport protocol. IPX provides the addressing system for the IPX/SPX stack. Operating at the Network and Transport layers of the OSI model, IPX directs the movement of packets on the internetwork using information it gains from the IPX Routing Information Protocol.

- **RIP (Routing Information Protocol)**—A routing protocol that uses two metrics—*clock ticks* (1/18 of a second) and hop count—to route packets through an IPX internetwork. IPX RIP (similar to TCP/IP RIP) is a distance vector routing protocol that builds and maintains routing tables between IPX-enabled routers and NetWare servers.

- **SAP (Service Advertisement Protocol)**—A protocol that advertises the availability of various resources on the NetWare network. NetWare servers broadcast SAP packets every 60 seconds, letting client machines on the network know where file and print services can be accessed (each type of service is denoted by a different hexadecimal number in the SAP packets).

- **NLSP (NetWare Link Services Protocol)**—A Novell developed link-state routing protocol that can be used to replace RIP (and SAP; more about the RIP SAP relationship in the section "Enabling and Configuring IPX Routing," later in this chapter) as the configured routing protocol for IPX routing.

IPX Addressing

For the exam, you also need to know about IPX addressing and how it provides both networking and node addressing information (and is in some respects similar to TCP/IP). IPX addressing uses an 80-bit (10 bytes) system, which is comprised of both network and node information, making it a hierarchical addressing system similar to IP addresses. IPX addresses appear in hexadecimal format and are broken down into two parts (see the following figure). The first part of the address, which can be up to 16 hexadecimal characters in length (this part of the address is 32 bits), is the *IPX network number*. The remaining 12 hexadecimal digits in the address make up the node address (which makes up the remaining 48 bits of the address).

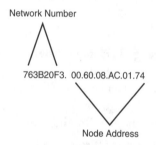

A NetWare segment on the network is often referred to as a wire, meaning a separate part of the overall data communication infrastructure. Wires are basically created when the first NetWare server on a particular segment is brought online. The server generates a network number for the wire during the server software installation. This hexadecimal number becomes the network number for the LAN (or segment or wire, if you prefer), no matter how many additional NetWare servers (additional file and print servers) are added to the LAN segment. So, all client machines (and additional servers) on the LAN will be assigned the same network number (such as 763B20F3, as shown in the previous figure).

When another new LAN (a separate segment or wire from the first LAN brought online) is brought into service, its network number will be provided by the first NetWare server brought online on that particular LAN. So, IPX networks are differentiated by their network numbers, whereas IP networks are differentiated by their subnet masks and the subnet bits in the IP addresses. Any routers that play a part in routing packets from a particular LAN (or wire) is configured with the network number for that NetWare segment. This means that if the Ethernet 0 interface on the router is connected to a particular NetWare LAN, it will use that LAN's network number in its interface configuration. Be advised for the exam that the NetWare administrator can edit the network number generated by the NetWare server. This gives the administrator the option of picking a simpler network address for the segment rather than having to remember and use the hexadecimal number generated by the server.

The node portion of the IPX address is actually dynamically assigned to the nodes on the network and consists of the MAC address on the network interface card. Therefore, an IPX address is the network number followed by the computer's MAC address.

SAP Broadcasts

One other aspect of NetWare that we must discuss before we can turn to the configuration aspects of IPX on a router is the part that SAP broadcasts play in IPX networking. The CCNA exam will pose questions about SAP because routers on a Novell network will build SAP tables just as Novell servers and clients do. This is how the routers share information related to the various wires or segments on the Novell network. To understand how a router builds its SAP table, you just have to look at the mechanism that the Novell servers use to share information related to the services on the segment.

Novell servers broadcast SAP announcements every 60 seconds. These broadcasts consist of all the services provided by the server making the SAP announcement and any other services the server has learned about that are provided by other NetWare servers. Where is the information a particular server has learned about other servers and the services they offer kept? It's logged in the server's SAP table.

When a particular server broadcasts a SAP advertisement, it is actually broadcasting its entire SAP table and is providing the SAP information to any server (or router) on the network that cares to listen. This means that the SAP information is shared among the servers. Clients on the various segments also use this SAP information to determine the location of print servers, file servers, and other resources on their particular wires.

Cisco routers that have interfaces configured for IPX also build SAP tables and broadcast their SAP information to the networks to which the router's interfaces are connected. Cisco routers do not, however, forward SAP broadcasts from one Novell LAN to another that are connected by a router (remember that routers are designed not to forward broadcast packets).

Instead, they do so by broadcasting their own SAP tables (which is a summary of the services offered by each LAN connected to a different router interface). The router then provides a summary of all the various LAN SAP tables to each of the different segments.

IPX

For the exam, it is also important for you to know the different encapsulation types for IPX and how IPX is configured on a Cisco router. As far as framing goes, remember that all data on a network is encapsulated in a particular frame type as it moves over the network media as a bitstream. Encapsulation is pretty straightforward with LAN protocols: Ethernet networks use an Ethernet frame; Token-Ring networks use a Token-Ring frame; and FDDI networks use an FDDI frame. However, NetWare supports more than one Frame type for the popular LAN architectures—Ethernet, Token-Ring, and FDDI. And if you don't configure your interfaces with the correct frame type or types, they aren't going to talk to nodes on the network or other routers on the internetwork.

NetWare actually supports four different frame types for Ethernet. Table 7.1 lists these frame types.

Table 7.1   Ethernet Frame Types

Frame Type	Where You Find It	Cisco IOS Keyword
Ethernet 802.3	Default Frame Type for early versions of NetWare(versions 2–3.11). This is the default frame type chosen when you enable IPX routing on the router.	`novell-ether`
Ethernet 802.2	Default Frame Type for NetWare versions 3.12–5.	`sap`

Table 7.1 continued

Frame Type	Where You Find It	Cisco IOS Keyword
Ethernet II	Used in networks running TCP/IP and/or DECnet.	arpa
Ethernet SNAP	Used in networks running TCP/IP and/or AppleTalk.	snap

Not only does Novell support more than one Ethernet frame type, but it also supports multiple Token-Ring and FDDI frames. For Token-Ring, it supports standard Token-Ring and Token-Ring Snap. For FDDI, it supports FDDI SNAP, FDDI 802.2, and FDDI RAW (FDDI frames that don't meet the IEEE specs).

You can specify multiple frame types—encapsulations—on a particular router interface, but each encapsulation must use a separate network number. You are, in effect, using different "virtual" networks to route the various frame types over an interface. To find the network number on a Novell server for a specific frame type, load the monitor utility on the server (type `load monitor` at the server prompt and then press Enter), and then open the Network information screens from the Monitor window.

Enabling and Configuring IPX Routing

IPX routing is enabled on the router using the global IPX routing command, which uses the syntax `ipx routing [node]`, where node is the MAC address of the interface. If you do not enter a node number (MAC address), it is entered automatically for you. Because serial interfaces do not have MAC addresses, they actually "borrow" the MAC address of one of the Ethernet ports on the router for IPX routing. After enabling IPX routing globally, you can then enable IPX on each interface that is connected to an IPX network:

1. At the privileged prompt, type **config t** and press Enter.

2. Type **ipx routing** at the configuration prompt, and then press Enter. After IPX routing is turned on "globally," you can configure individual interfaces.

3. To configure an Ethernet port for IPX (such as Ethernet 0), type **interface ethernet 0** at the configuration prompt and press Enter. The configuration prompt changes to `config-if`, letting you know that you can now enter the IPX information for the interface.

4. Type `ipx network` : `ipx network "network number" encapsulation "frame type"`, where `network number` is the NetWare network number provided to you by the NetWare administrator. You must also provide the encapsulation type in this compound command. Let's say that you are connecting an Ethernet interface to a Novell network running Novell Intranetware 4.11. This NOS uses the Ethernet 802.2 frame (Cisco IOS command sap). Therefore, a complete command would be `ipx network f87c2e0f encapsulation sap` (see the following figure). Press Enter to execute the command.

```
popeye#config t
Enter configuration commands, one per line.  End with CNTL/Z.
popeye(config)#ipx routing
popeye(config)#interface e0
popeye(config-if)#ipx network f87c2e0f encapsulation sap
popeye(config-if)#ipx network 76b20f3 encapsulation novell-ether sec
popeye(config-if)#^Z
popeye#
%SYS-5-CONFIG_I: Configured from console by console
popeye#
```

5. You can add a secondary IPX network address to a particular interface (using the sec designation for secondary). Use this command: `ipx network 76B20f3 encapsulation novell-ether sec`.

6. To complete the process and exit the configuration mode, press Ctrl+Z.

7. You might have to press Enter again to return to the privileged mode prompt.

Serial interfaces (using WAN protocols) are configured exactly the same way that you configure a LAN interface for IPX. Use the command `ipx network [ipx number] encapsulation [encapsulation type]`, in which `ipx number` is the network number for the interface and `encapsulation type` is one of the WAN protocols, such as PPP or HDLC.

Another subject that always seems to pop up on the exam is configuring an interface with more than one IPX link. If you want to configure your router to have more than one IPX link to the same path (meaning on a single router interface, which connects to a particular segment), use the global configuration command `ipx maximum-paths`. For example, you could use `ipx maximum-paths 2`.

Remember for the exam that, when you turn on IPX routing using the `ipx routing` command, this also automatically configures IPX RIP as the routing protocol. IPX RIP uses hop counts and clock ticks as the metric (the RIP used for IP routing used only hop counts). The way that the two metrics work together is pretty straightforward. If two paths that have the same hop count (let's say five hops) are found to a particular destination—using a router's IPX routing table—the more recent of the entries in the routing table (the path with the least number of clock ticks) is used as the route for the packets. The reverse is also true: When paths have the same tick count, the path with the fewest number of hops is chosen.

Monitoring IPX

You will also need to know how to monitor IPX on a Cisco router for the CCNA exam. Commands are available that enable you to view the IPX routing tables, IPX servers on various segments, and information related to routed IPX packets.

The IPX routing tables show the LANs (or segments) to which the router is directly connected and other segments that the router has learned about from other routers. You can enter the following command in the user or privileged mode: show ipx route. Next, press Enter. The following figure shows the result of this command.

```
popeye>show ipx route
Codes: C - Connected primary network,    c - Connected secondary network
       S - Static, F - Floating static, L - Local (internal), W - IPXWAN
       R - RIP, E - EIGRP, N - NLSP, X - External, A - Aggregate
       s - seconds, u - uses

3 Total IPX routes. Up to 1 parallel paths and 16 hops allowed.

No default route known.

C    763B20F3 (PPP),        Se0
C    F87C2E0F (SAP),        Et0
R    B86C033F [07/01] via 763B20F3.0010.7b3a.50c3,   53s, Se0
popeye>
```

To view the IPX configuration on a particular interface, such as an Ethernet 0 interface, you would type **show ipx interface Ethernet 0** and press Enter. The next figure shows the IPX information for Ethernet 0 on a 2505 router.

```
popeye#show ipx interface ethernet 0
Ethernet0 is up, line protocol is up
  IPX address is F87C2E0F.0010.7b3a.50b3, SAP [up]
  Delay of this IPX network, in ticks is 1 throughput 0 link delay 0
  IPXWAN processing not enabled on this interface.
  IPX SAP update interval is 1 minute(s)
  IPX type 20 propagation packet forwarding is disabled
  Incoming access list is not set
  Outgoing access list is not set
  IPX helper access list is not set
  SAP GNS processing enabled, delay 0 ms, output filter list is not set
  SAP Input filter list is not set
  SAP Output filter list is not set
  SAP Router filter list is not set
  Input filter list is not set
  Output filter list is not set
  Router filter list is not set
  Netbios Input host access list is not set
  Netbios Input bytes access list is not set
  Netbios Output host access list is not set
  Netbios Output bytes access list is not set
  Updates each 60 seconds, aging multiples RIP: 3 SAP: 3
  SAP interpacket delay is 55 ms, maximum size is 480 bytes
  RIP interpacket delay is 55 ms, maximum size is 432 bytes
  IPX accounting is disabled
  IPX fast switching is configured (enabled)
  RIP packets received 0, RIP packets sent 170
  SAP packets received 0, SAP packets sent 4
```

Several other show commands are also available for monitoring IPX activity and settings on the router. For the exam, make sure you know what type of information each command provides:

- **show ipx servers**—This command displays the contents of the router's SAP table, which lists the names of SAP services (such as file and print servers) on the IPX network.

- **show ipx traffic**—This command displays the number and type of IPX packets that have been transmitted and received by your router. Both RIP and SAP packet statistics are provided by this command.

- **show protocol**—This command displays the routed protocols enabled on the router and displays IPX address information for the router's interfaces (this command will also show the IP addresses of the router's interfaces if IP routing is enabled).

- **show ipx interface**—This command lists the interfaces enabled for IPX and then provides statistics on SAP and RIP broadcasts.

Another command that enables you to monitor IPX activity on the router is debug. The debug ipx routing activity privileged command is a little different in that it doesn't provide a static table of information like the show ipx route and show ipx traffic commands (those commands are similar to snapshots of the current status of the router). The debug ipx routing activity command actually lets you see the RIP and SAP broadcasts as your router sends and receives them (see the following figure). You must execute this command in the privileged mode.

Debugging requires a great deal of overhead on the router. To turn off debugging, use the command no debug ipx routing activity. The command no debug all turns off all debugging on the router.

TAKE THE TEST

This Practice Test provides you with questions related to two of the CCNA objectives from the "Networking Protocols" category "Novell IPX and IPX." These practice questions are structured the same as the questions that you will find on the exam.

1. Which of the following commands enables you to view the router's SAP table?

    A. `sh ipx route`

    B. `sh protocol`

    C. `sh ipx servers`

    D. `sh ipx traffic`

Answer A is incorrect; the `show ipx route` command provides the IPX routing table. Answer B is incorrect; the `show protocol` command provides a list of all routed protocols on the router. **Answer C is correct; the `show ipx servers` command displays the router's SAP table containing the SAP resources available on the various IPX networks.** Answer D is incorrect; the `show ipx traffic` command provides the number of types of IPX packets that have been sent and received by the router.

2. What constitutes the node portion of an IPX address?

    A. A number supplied by the administrator

    B. The network number provided by the NetWare server

    C. The MAC hardware address of the interface or NIC

    D. Random numbers generated by SAP broadcasts

Answer A is incorrect; the administrator can change only the network number on a NetWare server, not individual node numbers. Answer B is incorrect; the network number provided by the NetWare server is used as the network portion of the IPX address. **Answer C is correct; the MAC hardware address of an interface or the network card on a computer supplies the node portion of an IPX address. Serial interfaces "borrow" a node address from a LAN interface on the router.** Answer D is incorrect; SAP broadcasts provide only the location of resources, such as print servers, on a Novell segment.

3. Which of the following IPX/SPX protocols operates at the Network layer of the OSI model?

   A. NCP
   B. IPX
   C. SPX
   D. SAP

Answer A is incorrect; NCP handles the network functions at the Application, Presentation, and Session layers. **Answer B is correct; IPX is the Network layer protocol for the IPX/SPX stack.** Answer C is incorrect; SPX is the Transport layer protocol for the Novell stack. Answer D is incorrect; SAP is used to advertise resources on the NetWare wire.

4. The Cisco encapsulation keyword sap is actually which type of Ethernet frame?

   A. Ethernet 802.3
   B. Ethernet Snap
   C. Token-Ring Snap
   D. Ethernet 802.2

Answer A is incorrect; novell-ether is the Cisco keyword for the 802.3 frame. Answer B is incorrect; the Ethernet Snap Cisco keyword is snap. Answer C is incorrect; the keyword for Token-Ring Snap is token ring snap. **Answer D is correct; sap is the Cisco keyword for the Ethernet 802.2 frame type.**

5. To enable an interface with the IPX network 22af4 and an Ethernet II frame type, the command would read:

   A. ipx network 22af4 encap arpa
   B. ipx network encapsulation arpa
   C. ipx route 22af4 encapsulation arpa
   D. ipx network 22af4 encapsulation sap

Answer A is correct; the listed command supplies the correct network and frame type information, and `encap` is a valid abbreviation for encapsulation. Answer B is incorrect; the network number has not been supplied in the command. Answer C is incorrect; `ipx network`, not `ipx route`, sets the network number and encapsulation type. Answer D is incorrect; the encapsulation type of `sap` specified in the command does not set the correct frame type.

6. Which command would you use to show SAP and RIP updates on IPX-enabled interfaces?

   A. `sh ipx traffic`

   B. `sh ipx interface`

   C. `sh ipx servers`

   D. `sh ipx route`

Answer A is incorrect; this command shows the number and type of IPX packets sent and received by the router. **Answer B is correct; the `sh ipx interface` command provides SAP and RIP information on all IPX-enabled interfaces.** Answer C is incorrect; this displays the contents of the router's SAP table. Answer D is incorrect; this command shows the contents of the router's IPX routing table.

7. Which of these protocols provides connection-oriented transport to upper-layer protocols?

   A. IPX

   B. SAP

   C. RIP

   D. SPX

Answer A is incorrect; IPX is a connectionless Transport protocol providing the addressing system for IPX/SPX networks. Answer B is incorrect; SAP is an advertisement protocol advertising the availability of resources on the network. Answer C is incorrect; RIP is a routing protocol used on a NetWare network. **Answer D is correct; SPX operates at the Transport layer and provides connection-oriented services to upper-layer protocols.**

8. What is the node portion of the IPX address f87c2e0f.0010.7b3a.50b3?

   A. 50b3

   B. f87c2e0f

   C. 2e0f

   D. 0010.7b3a.50b3

Answer A is incorrect; everything after the first period in the address (going from the left) is part of the node address, and this only provides a portion of the node address. Answer B is incorrect; it provides the network portion of the address. Answer C is incorrect; it provides a portion of the network address (before the first period). **Answer D is correct; the number before the first period, f87c2e0f, is the network number; the rest of the address—the MAC hardware address for an interface—is the node address.**

Cheat Sheet

The Novell IPX/SPX protocol stack:

Protocol	Purpose
NCP	Provides network functions at the Application, Presentation, and Session layers
SPX	Connection-oriented protocol at the Transport layer that handles connection between sending and receiving nodes
IPX	Connectionless Network layer protocol that provides the addressing system for IPX.SPC packets
RIP	IPX/SPX Network layer routing protocol; uses hops and ticks as metrics
SAP	Upper-layer protocol that provides a mechanism for advertising and requesting services on a Novell segment
NLSP	Link state routing protocol at the Network layer designed to replace NetWare RIP

IPX Addressing:

network.node

The network portion of the address is generated by the first NetWare server brought online on the segment.

The node portion of the address is provided by the MAC address on the node's network interface card or on a router's LAN interface.

Example: f87c2e0f.0010.7b3a.50b3

Everything before the first period (f87c2e0f) is the network address.

Everything following the first period (0010.7b3a.50b3) is the node address.

SAP broadcasts provide a mechanism for advertising resources, such as file and print servers, on a Novell segment. Routers use SAP broadcasts from servers on the segment to build SAP tables.

SAP broadcasts take place every 60 seconds.

Novell supports multiple Ethernet frame types:

Frame Type	Cisco IOS Keyword
Ethernet 802.3	`novell-ether`
Ethernet 802.2	`sap`
Ethernet II	`arpa`
Ethernet SNAP	`snap`

Frame type mismatches result in communication problems on NetWare segments.

Novell IPX/SPX router commands:

Command	Result
`ipx routing`	Global configuration command that turns on IPX routing
`ipx network [ipx number]` `encapsulation` `[encapsulation type]`	Interface configuration command that enables the interface for IPX routing by specifying the IPX network number and encapsula tion type for the interface
`ipx maximum-paths 2`	Global configuration command that specifies the number of IPX links that can be configured for each IPX-enabled interface
`show ipx route`	Displays the IPX routing table for the router
`show ipx interface` `[interface type]` `[interface number]`	Displays the IPX configuration on the specified interface
`show ipx servers`	Displays the contents of the router's SAP table

Continued

Command	Result
show ipx traffic	Displays the number and type of IPX packets that have been transmitted and received by your router
show protocol	Displays the routed protocols enabled on the router
show ipx interface	Lists the interfaces enabled for IPX and provides statistics on SAP and RIP broadcasts
debug ipx routing activity	Privileged command that shows real-time IPX activity in the form of router updates and IPX traffic

Internetwork Routing

Cisco has divided its CCNA exam objectives into nine categories. Category 4 covers routing. Routing is one of the major topic categories for the exam, and a good understanding of routing, routing protocols, and how the router switches packets is required. One of the "Routing" category objectives, IGRP, is covered in this chapter. However, be advised that the exam guidelines are rather vague in several areas, routing in particular, so other material related to routing required to pass the exam is covered in this chapter. Routing has been added as a necessary objective to this chapter (although it appears as a category heading on the exam outline). This chapter also covers one topic in the "Cisco Basics, IOS, and Network Basics" category: Router Packet Switching Modes (see the following list of objectives).

- Routing
- IGRP
- Router Packet Switching Modes

19

Routing

Routers are internetworking devices that operate at the Network layer of the OSI model. Using a combination of hardware and software (Cisco routers use the Cisco internetwork operating system [IOS]), routers connect to networks. These networks can be Ethernet, Token-Ring, or FDDI—all that is required to connect these various network architectures is the appropriate interface on the router.

Because routers are Layer 3 devices, they take advantage of logical addressing to move packets between the various networks on the internetwork. Different switching modes are available for routing packets through an internetwork with routers and are discussed later in this chapter. Routers divide the enterprise-wide network into logical segments. On IP networks, these segments are referred to as *subnets* (as discussed in Chapter 6, "Network Protocols—TCP/IP").

Segmenting a network with a router provides several benefits in of itself and when compared to other internetworking devices such as bridges and switches. You should understand and know these benefits for the exam. One of the biggest benefits of using a router as opposed to a bridge or switch is that routers do not forward broadcast messages between the network segments, negating the possibility of a broadcast storm. A *broadcast storm* occurs when broadcast traffic (sometimes from malfunctioning devices, such as a bad network card) overcomes the network and swallows up all the available bandwidth. Broadcast storms are an inherent problem of Ethernet networks. Routers operate at the Network layer of the OSI model, enabling the administrator to use logical addressing to specify various network segments on the internetwork.

Routers can also be used to route more than one network protocol between the network segments. This provides the network administrator with a great deal of flexibility. A router can be configured to route IP, IPX, and AppleTalk simultaneously.

Routers also directly provide strategies for flow control. In addition, a router's capability to deal with congestion on the network and to be configured for redundant connections between devices enables the network administrator to design robust internetworks that are highly reliable.

In a nutshell, you need to know that routers provide greater flexibility and manageability when compared to bridges or switches. However, you should know that routers do have higher latency (the time it takes the router to process packets) than bridges or switches. For more about LAN segmentation at the Data Link layer of the OSI model, take a look at objective 34, "Network Segmentation and VLANs" in Chapter 12, "LAN Design and Segmentation."

Static Versus Dynamic Routing

Routers have two methods available for determining the routing of packets: static and dynamic. *Static* path determination, or static routing, simply means that the network administrator creates a table that supplies the static routes used to determine how the packets are switched on the internetwork as they move from source to destination. Static routing cannot react to any negative changes in the internetwork, such as a downed router or other line problem. Any changes to the static routes requires the network administrator to edit the static routing tables.

Cisco routers can be configured with static routes. The global configuration command syntax for a static route on an IP network is `ip route [network] [subnet mask] [default gateway]`. For example, to set up a static route for packets with a destination address that falls on the IP network 130.10.0.0, the global configuration command would be

```
ip route 130.10.0.0 255.255.0.0 130.10.20.1
```

In the previous command, `130.10.0.0` is the destination network, `255.255.0.0` is the subnet mask for the network, and `130.10.20.1` is the IP address of the router interface to which the packets should be switched (also known as the *default gateway* for the packets). This command would be repeated for each IP network until the entire static routing table was built for the internetwork.

More important in terms of the CCNA exam is *dynamic* routing, in which a routing protocol uses a metric(s) to build a routing table that provides the best path for routing packets on the internetwork. Dynamic routing means that the routers on the internetwork can react to downed interfaces and other route problems on the internetwork. Packets can be rerouted based on the dynamic routing tables, which are updated by the routers periodically.

In particular, you must know how to configure two routing protocols: RIP and IGRP (IGRP is covered in its own objective section later in the chapter). The *Routing Information Protocol (RIP)* is a distance vector routing protocol that uses hop count as its metric. A *hop* is the switching of packets from one router to another. Or in simpler terms, each time a router passes the packets off to the next router in the path, a hop has occurred.

RIP is the oldest IP routing protocol but is still in use today. It is also a typical distance vector routing protocol; RIP sends out a routing update message every 30 seconds, which consists of the router's entire routing table.

RIP is limited, however, in that the maximum number of hops it allows for the routing of packets is 15; 16 hops would be considered unreachable. This means that RIP is fine for smaller, homogenous internetworks but does not provide the metric flexibility necessary on larger networks. Why 15 hops? It's a design limitation of RIP.

Another limitation of RIP is the fact that it uses only one metric—hop count—and is therefore very single-minded when determining packet routing. It is incapable of taking the speed or reliability of the line into account when selecting packet paths. For example, in the following figure, even though Route A is the best path according to the number of hops (and RIP), you are forced to route your packets over a slower line (the 56KB leased line). This line is not only slow, but it also costs you money. Route B is actually over wire that the company owns (part of the network infrastructure) and is actually a faster medium (Ethernet at 10Mbps).

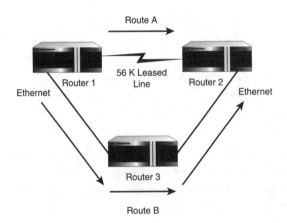

Configuring RIP

Configuring RIP is very straightforward. You must first select RIP as your routing protocol, and then designate the major network number for each interface you have enabled for IP routing.

1. At the Privileged prompt, type **config t** and press Enter. You are placed in the global configuration mode.

2. At the config prompt, type **router rip** and press Enter. This selects RIP as the routing protocol and changes the config prompt to the config-router prompt.

3. Type **network [major network number]** at the config-router prompt. major network number should be the network address for a Class A, B, or C network that is directly connected to the router.

4. Repeat the network [major network number] command for each IP network to which the router is directly connected. For example, in the following figure, two major networks (10.0.0.0 and 132.1.0.0—a Class A and Class B network, respectively) are connected to the router.

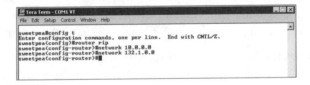

5. When you have finished entering the IP major networks connected to the router, press Ctrl+Z to exit the configuration mode (the command word end can also be used to exit the configuration mode).

One thing you should keep in mind for the exam is that IP routing must be enabled on the router by default. However, if IP routing has been disabled, you must enable it before you can configure a routing protocol, such as RIP. To enable IP routing on the router, use the global configuration command ip routing.

Viewing RIP Routing Tables and Other Parameters

RIP summarizes the information in the routing table by IP subnet numbers (also referred to as *network* numbers). To view the RIP routing table, use the command show ip route. The following figure shows the results of this command. Subnets marked with a C are subnets directly connected to the router; subnets marked with an R are routes RIP has learned.

You also can view only the subnets that RIP has learned by using RIP broadcasts received from neighboring routers. Use the command show ip route rip to view this subset of the complete routing table.

You can use the show ip protocol command to view the timing information related to RIP. For example, RIP updates are sent every 30 seconds, and the hold-down time for RIP is 180 seconds. This means that, if a router does not receive a RIP update from a connected router, it waits 180 seconds from the last received update and then flags the subnet path as suspect. After 240 seconds, the router actually removes the path information related to the other router from the routing table because it considers the path no longer usable.

If you want to view RIP update messages as they are sent and received by a router, you can use the Privileged command debug ip rip, as shown in the following figure.

To turn off RIP debugging, type **no debug ip rip** at the Privileged prompt and press Enter. Keep in mind that using debugging requires a fair amount of overhead from your router, so you should not leave debugging on for any lengthy period of time.

IGRP

The Interior Gateway Routing Protocol (IGRP) was developed by Cisco in the 1980s. IGRP is a distance-vector routing protocol. It uses a composite metric that takes into account several variables; it overcomes the limitations of RIP, such as the single hop count metric and the incapability of RIP to route packets on networks that require more than 15 hops. IGRP, on the other hand, has a hop limitation of 255 and was developed for larger internetworks.

IGRP's metric consists of a composite metric (meaning it takes several parameters into consideration when determining the best path) that takes into consideration bandwidth, delay, load, and reliability when determining the best route for data moving from a sending node to a particular destination node. The following list describes how each of these network parameters is viewed by IGRP when the routing protocol is used to build or update a router's routing table:

- Bandwidth is the capacity of a particular interface in kilobits—For example, a serial interface can have a bandwidth of 100,000Kb (this would be a serial interface connected to an ATM switch, which typically supplies this amount of bandwidth). Unfortunately, the bandwidth of a particular interface is not measured dynamically (measuring the actual bandwidth available at a particular time) but set statically by the network administrator using the interface configuration command bandwidth.

- Delay is the amount of time it takes to move a packet from the interface to the intended destination—Delay is measured in microseconds and is a static figure set by the network administrator using the interface configuration command delay. Several delays have been computed for common interfaces, such as Fast Ethernet and IBM Token-Ring. For example, the delay for a Fast Ethernet interface is 100 microseconds.

- Reliability is the ratio of expected to received keepalives—*Keepalives* are messages sent by network devices to let other network devices, such as a router, know that the link between them still exists on a particular router interface. Reliability is measured dynamically and is shown as a fraction when the show interface command is used on the router. For example, the fraction 255/255 represents a 100% reliable link.

- Load is the current amount of data traffic on a particular interface—Load is measured dynamically and is represented as a fraction of 255 (remember that 255 is the maximum number of hops through which IGRP can determine a path and is therefore used as a unit of measurement for reliability and load). For example, 1/255 would be an interface with a minimal amount of traffic, whereas 250/255 would be a fairly congested interface. Load can be viewed on the router using the show interface command.

IGRP sends updates every 90 seconds (as opposed to RIP's 30-second interval). Routes not confirmed for 630 seconds are flushed from the router's routing table.

Configuring IGRP

Configuring IGRP is similar to configuring RIP. You must enable the IGRP protocol and specify the major IP networks that are directly connected to the router's interfaces. However, because IGRP is used on larger internetworks (such as a complete corporate network), you must specify the autonomous system number for the autonomous system (AS) to which the router belongs. Several networks (Class A, B, or C) can be part of a particular autonomous system. Autonomous systems are tied together by core routers that run an Exterior Gateway Protocol, such as the Border Gateway Protocol. Follow these steps to configure IGRP:

1. At the Privileged prompt, type **config t** and press Enter. You are placed in the global configuration mode.

2. At the config prompt, type **router igrp [autonomous system number]**, in which autonomous system number is the AS number assigned to the AS to which your router belongs. After entering the command, press Enter.

3. Type **network [major network number]** at the config prompt. In this command, major network number is the network address for a Class A, B, or C network that is directly connected to the router.

155

4. Repeat the `network` [`major network number`] command for each IP network to which the router is directly connected (via its interfaces).

The following figure shows the steps for configuring IGRP on a router that belongs to an AS of 10. The `network` command has been used to enable advertisements to be sent and received by various router interfaces connected to different IP networks.

```
Tera Term - COM1 VT                                                     _ □ ✕
File  Edit  Setup  Control  Window  Help

sweetpea#config t
Enter configuration commands, one per line.  End with CNTL/Z.
sweetpea(config)#router igrp 10
sweetpea(config-router)#network 10.0.0.0
sweetpea(config-router)#network 132.1.0.0
sweetpea(config-router)#
```

Viewing IGRP Routing Tables and Other Parameters

You can view the IGRP routing table using the `show ip route` command. The following figure shows the results of this command. Networks marked with an "I" have been built into the routing table based on broadcast information from neighboring routers.

```
Tera Term - COM1 VT                                                     _ □ ✕
File  Edit  Setup  Control  Window  Help

Alice#sh ip route
Codes: C - connected, S - static, I - IGRP, R - RIP, M - mobile, B - BGP
       D - EIGRP, EX - EIGRP external, O - OSPF, IA - OSPF inter area
       E1 - OSPF external type 1, E2 - OSPF external type 2, E - EGP
       i - IS-IS, L1 - IS-IS level-1, L2 - IS-IS level-2, * - candidate default
       U - per-user static route

Gateway of last resort is not set

     10.0.0.0/8 is variably subnetted, 4 subnets, 2 masks
C       10.2.0.0/16 is directly connected, Serial0
C       10.2.1.1/32 is directly connected, Serial0
C       10.3.0.0/16 is directly connected, Ethernet0
I       10.1.0.0/16 [100/71544] via 10.2.1.1, 00:00:33, Serial0
I    132.1.0.0/16 [100/82125] via 10.2.1.1, 00:00:33, Serial0
Alice#
```

Two privileged `debug` commands also can be used to view IGRP update message parameters: `debug ip igrp events` and `debug ip igrp transaction`. The `debug ip igrp events` command provides a summary of IGRP updates as they are sent and received on the router's interfaces.

Conversely, the `debug ip igrp transaction` command provides a look at update messages sent and received and also provides a look at the composite metric or cost for each network connection (a number that is arrived at by combining all the metrics used). The following figure shows the results of the `debug ip igrp transaction` command.

```
Tera Term - COM1 VT
File Edit Setup Control Window Help
Alice#
IGRP: received update from 10.2.1.1 on Serial0
        subnet 10.1.0.0, metric 71544 (neighbor 1100)
        network 132.1.0.0, metric 82125 (neighbor 80125)
IGRP: sending update to 255.255.255.255 via Ethernet0 (10.3.1.1)
        subnet 10.2.0.0, metric=71444
        subnet 10.1.0.0, metric=71544
        network 132.1.0.0, metric=82125
IGRP: sending update to 255.255.255.255 via Serial0 (10.2.1.2)
        subnet 10.3.0.0, metric=1100
IGRP: received update from 10.2.1.1 on Serial0    subnet 10.1.0.0, metric 71544
(neighbor 1100)
        network 132.1.0.0, metric 82125 (neighbor 80125)
IGRP: sending update to 255.255.255.255 via Ethernet0 (10.3.1.1)
        subnet 10.2.0.0, metric=71444
        subnet 10.1.0.0, metric=71544
        network 132.1.0.0, metric=82125
IGRP: sending update to 255.255.255.255 via Serial0 (10.2.1.2)
        subnet 10.3.0.0, metric=1100
```

To turn off these debugging commands, type **no debug** followed by the rest of the appropriate command parameters. A quick way to turn off all debugging is by using the command no debug all.

Router Packet Switching Modes

This objective deals with the theory behind the two major modes or types of dynamic routing algorithms that can be used to determine the best path for packets switched by a router: distance-vector and link-state. You must understand the differences between these two types of routing protocols and the problems inherent with each type.

Distance-Vector Routing Protocols

Distance-vector routing protocols, such as RIP and IGRP, send out update messages at a prescribed time (RIP is every 30 and IGRP is every 90 seconds). A router using a distance-vector protocol passes its entire routing table to its neighboring routers (routers to which it is directly connected).

If a change occurs on the network, such as the addition of new routes or the loss of current routes, routers closest to the change update their routing tables. They then pass their tables onto their neighbors, who can then update their routing tables with the new information and pass it on to their nearest neighbors (and so on and so on).

Distance-vector routing tables can be likened to a line of dominos falling; each router in the sequence must update its table before it is passed on to its neighbor or neighbors. This causes a lag time to occur before all the routers on the internetwork contain updated routing tables. This lag time is also referred to as *convergence*.

Distance-vector routing tables provide information on how distance networks are reached via the various interfaces on a router. The following figure shows the routing table for the IGRP routing protocol.

```
Tera Term - COM1 VT
File  Edit  Setup  Control  Window  Help

Alice>sh ip route
Codes: C nected, S - static, I - IGRP, R - RIP, M - mobile, B - BGP
       D - EIGRP, EX - EIGRP external, O - OSPF, IA - OSPF inter area
       E1 - OSPF external type 1, E2 - OSPF external type 2, E - EGP
       i - IS-IS, L1 - IS-IS level-1, L2 - IS-IS level-2, * - candidate default
       U - per-user static route

Gateway of last resort is not set

     10.0.0.0/8 is variably subnetted, 4 subnets, 2 masks
C       10.2.0.0/16 is directly connected, Serial0
C       10.2.1.1/32 is directly connected, Serial0
C       10.3.0.0/16 is directly connected, Ethernet0
I       10.1.0.0/16 [100/71544] via 10.2.1.1, 00:00:20, Serial0
I     132.1.0.0/16 [100/82125] via 10.2.1.1, 00:00:20, Serial0
Alice>
```

Because of the way distance-vector protocols update routing tables, a possible problem that can arise is a routing loop. A *routing loop* occurs when routers on the network have not converged and invalid routes are still being sent in update messages. This means that packets are actually being switched based on incorrect information, causing them to "loop" through the routers on the internetwork without hope of reaching their final destinations.

While the packets loop through the internetwork, the hop count continues to increase. This is called *counting to infinity* and again is caused by the fact that the routing tables contain invalid information that points at a route that no longer exists.

Distance-vector problems, such as routing loops and counting to infinity, can be overcome with the following strategies:

- **Split Horizon**—Split horizon is used to solve the problem of counting to infinity in routing loops. Split horizon simply means that route information received in update messages on a particular interface cannot be advertised as part of any update messages sent out of the same interface. In essence, this means that incorrect routing information cannot ping-pong back and forth between two routers, setting up a routing loop.

- **Poison Reverse**—Route poisoning using poison reverse is another method of avoiding routing loops. When a particular route goes down, a router "poisons" its connection to the network by marking that network as unreachable. This means that incorrect routing updates cannot be received via that interface.

- **Hold-downs**—Hold-downs are used to make routers ignore update information for a set period of time. This means that changes will not be made to routing tables concerning the status of certain routes during the hold-down period. For example, if a route goes down, a router receiving an update message relaying this fact will mark the route as unreachable and start a hold-down timer. This route cannot be reinstated until the hold-down timer expires. This helps prevent incorrect information concerning that route coming from other routers from being added to the router's routing table.

For the exam, you must know the theory behind how distance-vector routing can avoid routing loops (as discussed here). You will not need to know how to actually implement the solutions, such as split horizon, poison reverse, and hold-downs.

Link-State Routing Protocols

Link-state routing protocols provide a topological database of all the links on the internetwork. This database includes information on routers, attached links, and neighbor routers. Therefore, link-state routing protocols provide a big-picture view of the network topology to routers instead of the "second-hand" perspective that distance-vector routing protocols provide a router (routers get their information from their neighbors). An example of a link-state protocol is the Open Shortest Path First (OSPF) routing protocol used for routing IP.

In effect, each router builds a complete map of the internetwork. Link-state routing protocols use link-state packets (LSPs) to inform routers on the internetwork of the state of these links. When a route changes, link-state advertisements enable routers to quickly recalculate a new best path for the routing of packets destined for a particular network. Routers using a link-state protocol have faster convergence than routers using distance-vector routing protocols.

Problems associated with link-state routing protocols have more to do with the resources they require than specific problems, such as the routing loops experienced by distance-vector routing protocols. Link-state protocols, however, use more router memory and router processor resources to build the complex network topology databases they use for routing.

Additionally, because link-state protocols send link-state packets to all the routers on the internetwork, a fair amount of bandwidth can be consumed by these messages. One way to overcome this frequent use of bandwidth is to change the timing of link status messages. By lengthening the period between messages, more bandwidth becomes available on the internetwork.

Multiprotocol Routing

Before ending this discussion of routing protocols, we should take a look at how Cisco defines the various types of multiprotocol routing. This topic has been known to pop up on the exam. *Multiprotocol* routing simply means that more than one LAN protocol can be routed on a router. In the case of separate multiprotocol routing, each routed LAN protocol has its own companion routing protocol that builds the routing table for the routed protocol.

For example, you could configure your router to route TCP/IP, IPX/SPX, and AppleTalk. Each of these routable protocols would require a different routing protocol—TCP/IP could use RIP or IGRP, IPX/SPX would use IPX RIP, and AppleTalk would use RTMP.

Each of the routing protocols builds its own routing table, unaware that other routing protocols are even running on the router. So, separate multiprotocol routing means just what it says: Multiple network protocols are routed separately, each using their own routing protocol.

Integrated multiprotocol routing is different from separate multiprotocol routing in that one routing protocol is capable of building routing tables for more than one routable network protocol. For example, the Enhanced Interior Gateway Routing Protocol (EIGRP) is actually capable of handling update messages and building routing tables for TCP/IP, IPX/SPX, and AppleTalk. A separate routing table is built for each LAN protocol, but only one routing protocol (namely, EIGRP) is used.

TAKE THE TEST

This Practice Test provides you with questions related to the "Routing" category, which includes IGRP as an objective. This practice exam also covers the Router Packet Switching Modes objective, which is found in the "Cisco Basics, IOS, and Network Basics" category. Because the exam is in a multiple-choice format, these questions are formatted as they would be on the actual exam.

1. RIP is a distance-vector routing protocol that uses _____ as its metric.

   A. Delay

   B. Bandwidth

   C. Hops

   D. Hold-downs

Answer A is incorrect; delay is one of the metrics used by IGRP for its composite metric. Answer B is incorrect; bandwidth is also an IGRP metric. **Answer C is correct; RIP uses hop count as its metric.** Answer D is incorrect; hold-downs are a method used to avoid routing loops when using distance-vector routing protocols.

2. Which configuration command is used to specify the network or networks that will be advertised when configuring RIP or IGRP?

   A. `router rip`

   B. `router igrp`

   C. `debug ip rip`

   D. `network [major network number]`

Answer A is incorrect; the `router rip` command selects RIP as the routing protocol. Answer B is incorrect; `router igrp` is used to select IGRP as the routing protocol, and it must be accompanied by an autonomous system number. Loop is the connection between the customer site and the CO. Answer C is incorrect; `debug ip rip` is a Privileged command used to view RIP update messages on the router. **Answer D is correct; after enabling RIP or IGRP, the major networks connected to the router must be specified using the `network` command.**

3. In terms of metrics used, RIP is a more sophisticated routing protocol than IGRP.

   A. True
   B. False

Answer A is incorrect; IGRP uses a composite metric consisting of bandwidth, delay, reliability, and load, providing more "intelligent" routing path determination than the one-metric RIP. **Answer B is correct; RIP uses only hop count as its metric and cannot determine whether the best path based on hops takes the best advantage of network bandwidth or route reliability as does IGRP.**

4. To view the complete IGRP routing table:

   A. Use the command `show igrp route`
   B. Use the command `show ip route igrp`
   C. Use the command `show ip route`
   D. Use the command `show ip route rip`

Answer A is incorrect; the command is incorrect—`show` must be followed by `ip route`. Answer B is incorrect; this command shows only the portion of the routing table built using update messages from neighboring routers. **Answer C is correct; this command shows the entire IP routing table.** Answer D is incorrect; this command shows a subset of the routing table for a router using RIP as the routing protocol.

5. To view IGRP routing update messages and the composite metric or cost for each connection:

   A. Use the `no debug all` command
   B. Use the `debug ip igrp events` command
   C. Use the `debug igrp transactions` command
   D. Use the `debug ip igrp transactions` command

Answer A is incorrect; this is the command used to turn off all debugging on the router. Answer B is incorrect; this command shows the update messages but does not provide the composite metric figure. Answer C is incorrect; the command syntax is wrong—the term ip must precede igrp in the command. **Answer D is correct; this command shows update messages and the composite metric or cost for each interface.**

6. An example of a routing protocol that provides integrated multiprotocol routing is

   A. RIP (for IP)

   B. EIGRP

   C. IGRP

   D. OSPF

Answer A is incorrect; RIP can be used to route only one routable protocol, IP. **Answer B is correct; EIGRP is capable of building routing tables for more than one routable protocol, such as IP, IPX, and AppleTalk.** Answer C is incorrect; IGRP can be used only to build routing tables for IP networks. Answer D is incorrect; OSPF can build routing tables only for IP networks.

7. A problem associated with distance-vector routing protocols is (select all that apply)

   A. Routing loops

   B. Processor and memory overhead

   C. Split horizon

   D. Slow convergence

Answer A is correct; routing loops are associated with distance-vector routing protocols. Answer B is incorrect; processor and memory overhead problems are associated with link-state routing protocols. Answer C is incorrect; split horizon is actually a method of dealing with routing loop problems. **Answer D is correct; the slower convergence time of distance-vector protocols can lead to routing loops.**

8. A benefit of segmenting a network with a router is

   A. Routers operate at the Data Link layer of the OSI model.

   B. Routers have a low latency period.

C. Routers do not forward broadcast messages, negating the possibility of a broadcast storm.

D. Routers can route only one network protocol at a time.

Answer A is incorrect; routers operate at the Network layer of the OSI model. Answer B is incorrect; routers have a higher latency period when compared to bridges or routers. **Answer C is correct; routers negate the possibility of broadcast storms.** Answer D is incorrect; routers can route multiple network protocols at the same time.

Cheat Sheet

Static routing means that a routing table is created statically by the network administrator.

Dynamic routing uses routing protocols that update their routing tables based on the conditions of internetwork connections.

RIP is a distance-vector routing protocol and uses hop count as its metric. Packets reaching a hop count of 16 are considered undeliverable. RIP sends update messages every 30 seconds by default.

To configure RIP (at the configuration prompt):

```
Router rip
network [major network number]
```

The `show ip protocol` command shows the RIP update period and the hold-down time for RIP (180 seconds).

The `debug ip rip` command provides a view of the routing updates sent and received by the router.

IGRP is a distance-vector routing protocol that uses a composite metric consisting of bandwidth, delay, load, and reliability.

To configure IGRP (at the configuration prompt), enter the following:

```
router igrp [autonomous system number]
network [major network number]
```

To view IGRP routing updates, use

```
debug ip igrp events
debug ip igrp transaction
```

`debug ip igrp transaction` provides composite metric for each route.

To view either the RIP or IGRP routing table:

```
show ip route
```

Separate multiprotocol routing means a separate routing protocol is used to build the routing table for each network protocol routed on the router.

Integrated multiprotocol routing means that one routing protocol builds separate tables for more than one routed network protocol. An example is EIGRP.

Routing protocol comparison:

Routing Protocol Type	Distance-Vector	Link-State
Problems	Routing loops, counting to infinity	Greater use of processor, memory, and bandwidth resources
Solutions	Split horizon, poison reverse, hold-downs	Increased period between link-state messages
Routing table	Based on information from neighboring routers	Topological map of entire network based on link-state advertisements

Benefits of segmenting networks with a router:

Router operates at Network layer, enabling division of network into logical subnetworks.

Routers do not forward broadcasts, negating the possibility of broadcast storms.

Routers provide flexibility to the administrator in that they can route multiple protocols through an interface.

Redundant connections can be provided, building fault tolerance into the internetwork.

WAN Protocols—HDLC Frame Relay and ATM

Cisco has divided its CCNA exam objectives into nine categories. Category 5 is "WAN Protocols." This chapter provides an introduction to Wide Area Networking, including information on important WAN protocols that you need to know for the exam. I have added an objective to this chapter called WAN Protocols Overview, which provides a short summary of the important WAN protocols (in terms of the exam). This chapter also covers three specific objectives of the "WAN Protocols" category: HDLC, Frame Relay, and ATM (see the following list).

- WAN Protocols Overview
- HDLC
- Frame Relay
- ATM

22

WAN Protocols Overview

Expanding the corporate enterprise across distances (both great and small) requires technology that can be used to connect company LANs (which is an infrastructure owned by the company) at various locations. Wide area network (WAN) technology provides the capability to connect networks using a service provider, such as the public telephone system or other private switched network that provides the necessary infrastructure for the movement of data between the corporate LAN sites.

Several WAN protocols are available for moving data over private and public networks, including Frame Relay, ATM, ISDN/LAPD, HDLC, and PPP. Each of these WAN protocols is discussed in the following sections.

Frame Relay

Frame Relay is a Data Link packet switching protocol that provides communications between local area networks. Frame Relay was originally developed for use over ISDN lines but can now be used in several implementations.

Frame Relay actually uses packets of varying sizes and takes advantage of permanent virtual circuits that provide dedicated connections between networks communicating over the switched network. We will discuss Frame Relay in greater detail later in the chapter.

ATM

Asynchronous Transfer Mode (ATM) is a high-speed, packet switching protocol used in WAN environments. ATM uses fixed-length data packets called *cells*, which speeds transmission rates. Each cell is 53 bytes. ATM WAN networks, which exist as both private ATM networks and public ATM networks (through a service provider, such as the telephone company) employ permanent virtual circuits between connecting points on the network and can theoretically achieve speeds of 1.2Gbps.

An important aspect of ATM switches (for the exam) is that ATM technology has been adapted to the LAN environment and is employed for high-speed network backbones. ATM WAN deployments also have recently become important as Digital Subscriber Line technology (data over regular phone lines) has become increasingly available to businesses and individuals seeking higher-speed Internet connections. ATM and its LAN implementation are discussed in greater detail later in this chapter.

ISDN/LAPD

ISDN (Integrated Services Digital Network) is a digital service that runs over the existing phone lines. ISDN consists of protocols and standards defined by the ITU (International Telephone Union). It comes in two types—Basic Rate ISDN (BRI) and Primary Rate ISDN (PRI)—and supports both data and voice transmissions.

The ISDN protocols and standards span the Physical, Data Link, Network, and Transport layers of the OSI model; however, ISDN is a little different from the other WAN protocols discussed in this chapter. ISDN is actually the physical conveyance of the data as it moves from a router to the Public Switched Telephone network. It is not the encapsulation type, so you still must specify an encapsulation type, such as HDLC, PPP, or Frame-Relay.

ISDN supplies two channel types: B Channels and D Channels (which are discussed further in the next chapter). LAPD (Link Access Procedure on the D channel) is a Data Link layer protocol that is part of the signaling standards for the Basic Rate ISDN (which you will configure in the next chapter).

Point-to-Point Protocols

You also must differentiate between two point-to-point protocols for serial communication on the router—HDLC (High-Level Data Link Control protocol) and PPP (Point-to-Point protocol). The configuration of these protocols is discussed in the next chapter.

HDLC is a point-to-point WAN protocol that operates at the Data Link layer and serves as the default WAN protocol on Cisco routers. It is used for synchronous serial connections over dedicated lines and ISDN. More about HDLC is discussed in the next section.

PPP, a Data Link layer protocol, is widely used as the protocol for connecting dial-up connections to TCP/IP networks, such as the Internet. PPP can be used over asynchronous (dial-up) or synchronous lines. Because PPP is part of the TCP/IP open system, it is consistent across various manufacturers' devices. PPP supports data compression and provides authentication using either the Password Authentication Protocol (PAP) or Challenge Handshake Authentication Protocol (CHAP). PPP is discussed in more detail in Chapter 10, "WAN Protocols—Configuring PPP and ISDN."

HDLC

The High-Level Data-Link Control (HDLC) protocol is the default point-to-point protocol for WAN interfaces on Cisco routers. The HDLC protocol on Cisco routers is a propriety version of the protocol and therefore cannot be used to communicate with routers from other manufacturers that also deploy HDLC. (PPP, being standard on all routers, would typically be used in situations where non-Cisco equipment is deployed with Cisco equipment.)

HDLC is a bit-synchronous, Data Link layer WAN protocol. It actually came into being when the International Standard Organization (ISO) modified the Synchronous Data-Link Control protocol developed by IBM for their Systems Network Architecture (SNA) environments involving IBM main-frame and mini-frame technologies. HDLC was further developed by the International Telecommunication Union Telecommunication Standardization Sector (ITU-T) and the IEEE, which resulted in the IEEE 802.2 standard.

When configuring HDLC on the router (which should be enabled on the WAN interfaces on an unconfigured router), the only other parameter you might need to provide is the bandwidth for the WAN connection. But this is required only in cases in which the network routing protocol is IGRP, which uses bandwidth as one of its metrics. If HDLC is not the current WAN protocol for a particular interface, it is also quite easy to enable it on a serial interface.

Remember that the bandwidth is the throughput for the WAN line you have leased from your WAN provider. For example, a 56KB line would have a bandwidth of 56—bandwidth is measured in kilobits/second. On the router, the WAN interface command bandwidth 56 would set the appropriate throughput for this connection. Follow these steps:

1. At the privileged prompt, type config t and press Enter. You are placed in the global configuration mode.

2. To configure a particular WAN interface, type the name of the interface at the prompt, such as `interface serial 1`. Then press Enter. The prompt changes to the config-if mode.

3. Type **encapsulation HDLC** and press Enter.

4. If you need to set the bandwidth for the interface, type **bandwidth [kilobits/second]**, where `kilobits/second` is the speed of the line. For example, for a 56KB line, the command would be **bandwidth 56**. Then, press Enter. In the following figure, HDLC is set as the WAN protocol using the `encapsulation` command. Use the `bandwidth` command to set the bandwidth if necessary.

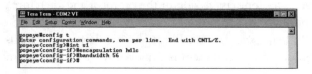

5. To end the configuration of the interface, either press Ctrl+Z or type **end** and press Enter.

HDLC is often deployed in dial-on demand routing (DDR) situations, where an expensive leased line such as an ISDN line is used as a backup connection for the routed network. This use of redundant "emergency" connections builds fault tolerance into the routed network (keep this in mind for the exam).

Frame Relay

Before discussing the actual features of Frame Relay, be advised that you also must know the terminology that is used to describe your corporate LAN equipment, the phone company's equipment, and the point where your equipment ends and their equipment begins in the context of a Frame Relay WAN. The following figure provides a diagram of a Frame Relay connection between two routers. A Frame Relay WAN connection consists of customer equipment and equipment provided by the service provider. Definitions of important WAN terms follow the diagram.

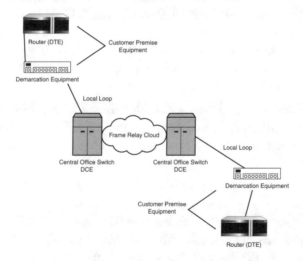

- **Customer Premise Equipment (CPE)**—The equipment (both the LAN equipment and the leased WAN equipment at the customer's site).
- **Data Terminal Equipment (DTE)**—Typically, the router that terminates your LAN and is configured with the WAN protocol.
- **Data Communication Equipment (DCE)**—The device that takes the LAN data and moves it across the switched network, such as a Frame

Relay switch. Modems and other devices such as a DSU/CSU (Data Services Unit/Channel Services Unit) are also considered DCE devices.

- **Central Office (CO)**—The provider's nearest switching facility (in relation to your LAN location).

- **Local Loop**—The cabling that runs from the customer's site to the nearest CO.

- **Demarcation**—The point where the customer's premise equipment ends and the local loop begins.

- **Frame Relay Cloud**—The actual switched network that provides the movement of data between the DTEs on each LAN.

As already mentioned, Frame Relay is a packet switching protocol that operates on a WAN. Frame Relay connections use DTEs and DCEs (with the DCE providing the connection from a DTE, such as a router, to the actual WAN connection). DCE devices on Frame Relay networks consist of the carrier owned switches.

Frame Relay uses permanent virtual circuits (PVC) for communication sessions between points on the WAN (the connected DTEs). These PVCs are identified by a Data Link connection identifier (DLCI)—a value provided by the Frame Relay service provider. PVCs are used because they provide an active communication session for recurring communications between two points on the WAN.

Because several virtual circuits can exist on a corporate WAN using Frame Relay, multiple DLCIs can be configured on one interface using subinterfaces. This enables one router to connect to several routers over one interface using several different PVCs.

A set of enhancements was added to the Frame Relay protocol by Cisco, Northern Telecom, and others—called LMI (Local Management Interface). LMI is the signaling standard used between the router and the Frame Relay switch and provides information such as the global significance of the DLCI virtual circuits and the status of the virtual circuits. Cisco routers support three LMI types:

- **Cisco**—Cisco, Northern Telecom, DEC, and StrataCom LMI type
- **ANSI**—American National Standards LMI type
- **Q933A**—International Telecommunications standard LMI type

The default LMI type for a Cisco router is cisco. LMI autosense became available with IOS version 11.2; the router tries to autodetect the LMI type that is being used on the line between the router and switch. It sends a request to the Frame Relay switch, which then responds with the LMI type or types for the line. The router then autoconfigures itself using the last LMI type that it receives from the switch. As far as the exam goes, know the various LMI types and the fact that cisco is the default.

Configuring Frame Relay

When you configure Frame Relay on a router's serial interface, you must set the encapsulation type and provide the DLCI number (which defines the permanent virtual circuit) for the interface. And although IOS version 11.2 (and newer) autosenses the LMI type, it's a good idea to know the configuration commands for setting the LMI type on a router for the CCNA exam. DLCIs have only local significance, whereas LMI has global significance.

Frame Relay Encapsulation and DLCIs

Frame Relay is set as the encapsulation type at the interface configuration prompt. By default, the Frame Relay encapsulation you set up on a serial interface is set up to connect two Cisco routers across the WAN. If you must connect a Cisco router to non-Cisco DTE equipment across a WAN, you must use the Internet Engineering Task Force (IETF) parameter (directly following the encapsulation frame-relay command). The following figure shows the command set for specifying Frame Relay encapsulation on a serial interface. It is important that both local and remote routers have the same LMI type for the Frame Relay circuit to be active.

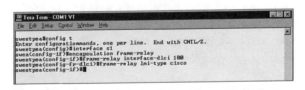

To set the DLCI for the router interface, you use the command frame-relay interface-dlci [#], where the number is the DLCI number of the interface. The DLCI number is provided by the service provider and is a number in the range 16–1007. The figure also provides a look at setting the DLCI for the interface, where 100 has been specified as the DLCI number.

177

The LMI is set for the router interface using the command `frame-relay interface-lmi [type]`, where `type` is Cisco, ANSI, or Q933a. As already mentioned, the LMI type is autodetected by routers using IOS 11.2 or better.

Mapping Network Protocol Addresses

Other parameters can also be configured in relation to Frame Relay, such as IP address-to-DLCI mappings. Network devices at the end of the Frame Relay connections require that their network addresses be mapped to the DLCI on the interface if they are going to successfully communicate over the WAN connection. For example, the IP address of the interface would need to be mapped to the appropriate DLCI. This can be done either by using the Inverse Address Resolution Protocol (Inverse ARP)—which dynamically maps IP addresses to DLCIs—or by creating static mappings between IP addresses and DLCIs.

When you use the `encapsulation frame-relay` command at the interface configuration prompt, Inverse ARP is set up by default to handle the IP-to-DLCI mappings. You can configure your own mappings using the `frame-relay map` command. You should use `map ip` statements only if no `frame-relay inverse-arp` command has been issued.

The syntax for the `map` command is `frame-relay map [network protocol] [address] [DLCI number] [encapsulation or other parameter]`, where the `network protocol` is IP or IPX (or some other network protocol) and the `address` is the interface address, such as the IP address followed by the DLCI number. An additional parameter can be added to the end of the command, such as the Frame Relay encapsulation type (cisco or ietf). The following figure shows the `map` command for a serial interface. The `help` command has been used to show the additional parameters that can optionally be added to the end of the command. This is equivalent to issuing a static route in IP; the local router must know which route to take to reach the destination. When you issue the `map ip` statement, you are providing this information.

```
Tera Term - COM1 VT

File  Edit  Setup  Control  Window  Help

sweetpea(config-if)#frame-relay map ip 10.12.1.1 100 ?
  broadcast            Broadcasts should be forwarded to this address
  cisco                Use CISCO Encapsulation
  compress             Enable TCP/IP and RTP/IP header compression
  ietf                 Use RFC1490/RFC2427 Encapsulation
  nocompress           Do not compress TCP/IP headers
  payload-compression  Use payload compression
  rtp                  RTP header compression parameters
  tcp                  TCP header compression parameters
  <cr>
```

Configuring Subinterfaces

Your serial interfaces can be configured with multiple subinterfaces. This enables you to configure each subinterface as if it were a separate hardware interface. This is particularly useful when you have multiple DLCIs associated with an interface—you can create a subinterface for each DLCI.

Subinterfaces also can be configured with their own network protocols. For example, you could create two subinterfaces on your serial 0 interface and configure one of the subinterfaces for IP and the other for IPX.

Subinterfaces are created at the global configuration prompt. To create a subinterface on serial 0, you use the command int s0.[number] point to point or multipoint. In this command, the number is the subinterface number followed by the type of subinterface: either point-to-point or multipoint. Remember, however, that an interface must be encapsulated for Frame Relay before you can create subinterfaces on that WAN interface.

Point-to-point is used when a single PVC connects two DTEs, and multipoint is used in a situation where you have a PVC mesh and multiple PVCs are available. The following figure shows the creation of a subinterface and the assignment of a DLCI to the subinterface. The subinterface number used was the same as the DLCI for the subinterface.

```
sweetpea(config)#int s1.200 point-to-point
sweetpea(config-subif)#frame-relay interface-dlci 200
sweetpea(config-fr-dlci)#
```

Monitoring Frame Relay

Several show commands are available for viewing Frame Relay configuration settings and statistics. The show interface command provides all the configuration statistics for an interface and also shows the DLCI type (but not the number) and the LMI type for the interface.

The show frame-relay lmi command provides the LMI type and a listing of invalid messages that have been sent or received by the router. It also shows the valid LMI messages that have been sent and received. The following figure shows the result of this command.

```
popeye#show frame-relay lmi

LMI Statistics for interface Serial0 (Frame Relay DCE) LMI TYPE = ANSI
    Invalid Unnumbered info 0         Invalid Prot Disc 0
    Invalid dummy Call Ref 0          Invalid Msg Type 0
    Invalid Status Message 0          Invalid Lock Shift 6
    Invalid Information ID 0          Invalid Report IE Len 0
    Invalid Report Request 0         Invalid Keep IE Len 0
    Num Status Enq. Rcvd 60           Num Status msgs Sent 54
    Num Update Status Sent 0          Num St Enq. Timeouts 5
```

The show frame-relay map command provides the map table for your Frame Relay interfaces. The mapping of network protocol addresses to DLCI numbers are listed in the map table (see the following figure). Remember that the map table can be configured dynamically (using Inverse ARP) or statically mapped using the frame-relay map command. When you issue this command, you are confirming end-to-end connectivity on the interface.

```
popeye#sh frame map
Serial0 (up): ip 130.10.64.2 dlci 100(0x64,0x1840), dynamic,
              broadcast,, status defined, active
Serial0 (up): ipx 763B20F3.0010.7b3a.50c3 dlci 100(0x64,0x1840), dynamic,
              broadcast,, status defined, active
Serial0 (up): appletalk 11.45 dlci 100(0x64,0x1840), dynamic,
              broadcast,, status defined, active
popeye#
```

The show frame-relay pvc command provides the DLCI number of the PVC, the type of PVC (local or global), and the PVC status. Remember for the exam that only this command and the show interface command provide the DLCI numbers.

Two additional commands that you should be familiar with are show frame relay route and show frame-relay traffic. show frame relay route provides the input and output statistics for each DLCI; the show frame-relay traffic command provides statistics for the protocols running on the router related to Frame Relay traffic, such as IP.

ATM

As mentioned earlier in this chapter, ATM is a WAN packet-switching technology that uses a 53-byte cell to move data across public and private wide area networks. The ATM protocol stack consists of protocols that reside at the Data Link and Physical layers of the OSI model. ATM networks support the *multiplexing* of information, which is the combining of several channels of information into one data stream. ATM networks also provide a network medium for carrying voice, video, and data traffic.

ATM provides a connection-oriented environment and uses a virtual channel as the connection between a sending and a receiving device. A *virtual channel* is equivalent to the virtual circuit used for Frame Relay. A bundle of virtual channels is referred to as a *virtual path* (when you configure these on the router, they are called PVCs—permanent virtual circuits—just as they were for Frame Relay. Virtual channels are identified on the WAN by a virtual path identifier and virtual channel identifier.

For the exam, be aware that ATM is typically deployed over high-speed, fiber-optic networks (although in a LAN environment, which we will discuss shortly, ATM can be run over twisted-pair wire). For example, Synchronous Optical Network/Synchronous Digital Hierarchy (SONET, as it is typically known) is one of the Physical layers for ATM. SONET can provide a throughput of 155Mbps over multimode fiber cabling.

As far as hardware goes, ATM wide area networks consist of two devices: ATM switches and ATM endpoints. The ATM *switch* moves the data from a LAN through the WAN cloud to another ATM switch and the data's final destination. An ATM *endpoint* is any device that terminates the local area network and provides the connection to the ATM switch. Routers, digital service units (DSUs), and LAN switches can all serve as ATM endpoints. For the exam, you must know that routers can serve as endpoints and how a router's WAN interface is configured for ATM. This is discussed in the next section.

Configuring ATM

ATM can be configured on a router's serial interface in much the same way that protocols such as HDLC and Frame Relay are configured. It is assumed that the router's serial interface is connected to an ADSU—an ADSU is a terminal adapter used to access an ATM network.

The serial interface should be enabled for the protocol it will carry. For example, if IP is to be routed over the serial interface, the interface should be assigned an IP address. Then, you must set the encapsulation type for the serial interface and provide other parameters related to the WAN protocol used, in this case ATM.

The encapsulation type for ATM is ATM-DXI. *DXI* (Data Exchange Interface) is control information in the form of a header that is placed on packets sent by the router to the ADSU. It provides the ADSU with a confirmation that the router is enabled as a network endpoint for ATM. The ADSU then simply strips the DXI header off the packets and sends them on their way to the ATM network.

The interface configuration command for ATM encapsulation is `encapsulation atm-dxi`. After the ATM encapsulation type is set at the `config-if` prompt, the PVC for the ATM connection can be set.

The PVC is created by the interface configuration command `dxi pvc [vpi #] [vci #] [snap, nlpid, or mux]`. `vpi #` is the virtual path identifier supplied for the connection by your ATM service provider. `vci #` is the virtual channel identifier for the connection, again, supplied by your ATM service provider.

The final parameter in the command, which consists of `snap`, `nlpid`, or `mux`, needs a little more clarification. This parameter controls options related to the number of LAN protocols that the PVC can switch (such as TCP/IP, IPX/SPX, and so on).

SNAP (Subnetwork Access Protocol) enables you to set up the PVC so that it can carry multiple protocols. SNAP is the default. *NLPID (network layer protocol identification)* also allows multiple LAN protocols on the PVC and is provided only to supply backward compatibility with earlier versions of the Cisco IOS (versions prior to 10.3). With version 11.3 of the IOS (which the CCNA exam covers), SNAP would be used. The `mux` (which is an abbreviation for multiplexor) option sets up the PVC to handle only one network protocol. This is used in situations in which multiplexors are used to combine channels over a T1 or other high-speed line that provides access to the ATM WAN.

So, say you want to configure a PVC for ATM where you were assigned a VPI of 20 and a VCI of 15 (the numbers don't have an actual value, they are different for each ATM service provider and serve as mappings for their WAN PVCs) and want to route multiple network protocols over the ATM connection. The command would look like the following:

```
dxi pvc 20 15
```

Notice that SNAP was not added to the end of the command. Because it is the default, you do not need to specify that parameter. SNAP would be used to provide the routing of multiple protocols over the PVC. In a case where you will route only one protocol over the ATM connection's PVC, the command would be

```
dxi pvc 20 15 mux
```

After you have set the ATM encapsulation type for the serial interface and provided the PVC information, you end the configuration setting by pressing Ctrl+Z. Saving your configuration settings to the startup configuration of the router is important. This is accomplished with the copy run start command.

Monitoring ATM

For the exam, you also should know how to monitor ATM configurations on your router's serial interfaces. Two commands are particularly useful:

- show interfaces atm—This command shows the status of configured ATM interfaces on the router.
- show dxi pvc—This command provides the configuration information for ATM PVCs on the router.

ATM LAN Implementations

Because of their capability to move data at high speeds, ATM switches have been ported over to the LAN environment and are used as an alternative to other technologies such as FDDI for high-speed backbones on large local area networks. Because Cisco manufactures ATM switches, you must remember (for the exam) that ATM can be implemented in the LAN environment (as well as the WAN environment we discussed earlier).

ATM switches that are deployed on a LAN (meaning workstations, routers, and LAN switches can be directly connected to these ATM switches) use LAN Emulation (LANE) to emulate a LAN on top of the ATM network. This is accomplished by the LANE protocol, which can emulate either an Ethernet or a Token-Ring network.

The LANE protocol is capable of emulating a LAN Data Link protocol by defining a service interface at the Data Link layer of the OSI model. This provides the same services to the Network layer that would normally be performed by MAC sublayer protocols defined by the IEEE specifications 802.3 (Ethernet) and 802.5 (Token-Ring). So, the fact that ATM switches are on the LAN is transparent to all the other devices, such as servers, clients, and LAN switches. The LAN operates just as a typical Ethernet or Token-Ring network would operate; however, it runs at a much higher speed because of the ATM switches. Although the CCNA exam does not require that you know how to configure ATM switches for LAN Emulation, remember that test questions related to why and how LAN Emulation can be implemented on ATM switches will probably appear on the exam.

TAKE THE TEST

This Practice Test provides you with questions related to three objectives from the "WAN Protocols" category: HDLC, Frame Relay, and ATM. Questions related to general WAN information that you will need to know for the exam and was covered in this chapter are also included. Because the CCNA exam is in a multiple-choice format, these questions are formatted as they would be on the actual exam.

1. If you needed to connect a Cisco router to a non-Cisco device point-to-point over a synchronous connection, which protocol would you use?

   A. HDLC
   B. PPP
   C. ISDN
   D. IP

Answer A is incorrect; HDLC is a proprietary Cisco protocol. **Answer B is correct; PPP is consistent across various "brands" of connectivity devices.** Answer C is incorrect; ISDN is a digital service and would require an encapsulation type. Answer D is incorrect; IP is a network protocol, not a WAN protocol.

2. When speaking in terms of WAN connectivity, the equipment that your company owns is referred to as the

   A. CO
   B. Local loop
   C. CPE
   D. Frame Relay cloud

Answer A is incorrect; the CO, or central office, is the nearest provider switching office. Answer B is incorrect; the local loop is the connection between the customer site and the CO. **Answer C is correct; the CPE, or customer premise equipment, is the equipment that is part of your corporate infrastructure.** Answer D is incorrect; the Frame Relay cloud refers to the packet switched public or private network used to move the packets.

3. The PVC for a router interface configured with Frame Relay is designated by a

   A. LMI type

   B. Subinterface

   C. DLCI

   D. Frame Relay encapsulation—cisco/ietf

Answer A is incorrect; the LMI type relates to the signaling standard for the Frame Relay connection. Answer B is incorrect; subinterfaces are used for convenient mapping of multiple PVCs to a router interface. **Answer C is correct; a PVC is identified by a DLCI number.** Answer D is incorrect; Frame Relay encapsulation is either cisco by default or can be configured as ietf for connecting to non-Cisco devices.

4. To set the DLCI number for a router subinterface called s1.200, the command sequence would be

   A. `config t, frame-relay interface-dlci [#]`

   B. `config t, int s1, encap frame-relay`

   C. `config t, int s1.200 encap frame-relay`

   D. `config t, int s1, encap frame-relay, int s1.200 point-to-point, frame-relay interface-dlci [#]`

Answer A is incorrect; the `frame-relay dlci` command must be used at the interface or subinterface configuration prompt. Answer B is incorrect; this command sets only the serial interface encapsulation type as Frame Relay. Answer C is incorrect; this command cannot be used at the subinterface level. **Answer D is correct; you must encapsulate the Serial 1 interface as Frame Relay, create the subinterface, and then specify the DLCI for the subinterface.**

5. The Frame Relay LMI types for a Cisco router interface are (select all that apply)

   A. IETF

   B. ANSI

   C. Q933A

   D. Cisco

Answer A is incorrect; IETF is actually a Frame Relay encapsulation type for connecting to non-Cisco devices across a Frame Relay connection. **Answers B, C, and D are correct; ANSI, Q933a, and Cisco are LMI standards.**

6. Which of the following commands shows the DLCI number for a serial interface (select all that apply)?

   A. `show frame-relay lmi`

   B. `show frame-relay map`

   C. `show interface`

   D. `show frame-relay pvc`

Answer A is incorrect; this command shows the LMI statistics for Frame Relay interfaces. **Answer B is correct; `frame-relay map` shows the DLCI numbers and their mapping to network protocol addresses.** Answer C is incorrect; the `show interface` command shows encapsulation types and other Frame Relay statistics but on the DLCI number. **Answer D is correct; this command provides the PVC statistics and the DLCI numbers.**

7. A subinterface that has been created for a serial interface that will provide only one PVC connection to a remote site should be configured as

   A. Multipoint

   B. IETF

   C. Point-to-point

   D. Q933A

Answer A is incorrect; multipoint is used to configure the subinterface when multiple PVCs are available in a mesh. Answer B is incorrect; IETF is a Frame Relay encapsulation type used to connect to non-Cisco equipment. **Answer C is correct; subinterfaces connecting via one PVC are configured as point-to-point.** Answer D is incorrect; Q933A is one of the LMI types for a Frame Relay interface.

187

8. The `frame-relay map` command can be used to map DLCIs to which of the following (select all that apply):

A. IP addresses

B. IPX addresses

C. AppleTalk addresses

D. Subinterfaces

Answers A, B, and C are correct; the `frame-relay map` command is used to map network protocol addresses to DLCI numbers. Answer D is incorrect; DLCIs are assigned to interfaces and subinterfaces using the `frame-relay interface-dlci#` command.

9. The ATM PVC command `dxi pvc` requires that two parameters be provided by the ATM service provider; they are

A. The LANE protocol number

B. The VCI number

C. The encapsulation type

D. The VPI number

Answer A is incorrect; the LANE protocol is used in ATM LAN emulations and is not assigned a number. **Answer B is correct; the Virtual Channel Identifier (VCI) must be provided by the service provider to configure the PVC for the WAN connection.** Answer C is incorrect; the encapsulation type must be set with the `encapsulation atm-dxi` command before you can create the PVC for the interface, and the encapsulation type must be `atm-dxi`. **Answer D is correct; the Virtual Path Indicator (VPI) must also be provided by the ATM service provider.**

10. Which command provides configuration information for ATM PVCs on a router?

A. show frame-relay pvc

B. show interfaces atm

C. show interfaces

D. show dxi pvc

Answer A is incorrect; this command provides configuration information on Frame Relay PVCs. Answer B is incorrect; this command shows the status of an ATM interface on the router. Answer C is incorrect; this command provides information on all the interfaces on the router but does not provide

PVC configuration information. **Answer D is correct; the** `show dxi pvc` **command provides PVC configuration information for ATM interfaces.**

Cheat Sheet

WAN technology and protocols enable network administrators to connect LANs at different geographical locations.

Frame Relay is a packet-switching protocol that uses permanent virtual circuits to move data across a public or private switched network.

ISDN is a digital service that runs over the existing phone lines and supports both data and voice transmissions.

HDLC is a proprietary Cisco point-to-point protocol that provides WAN connectivity over synchronous lines.

PPP is a point-to-point protocol that provides connectivity over both asynchronous and synchronous lines.

Frame relay terms:

- Permanent Virtual Circuit (PVC)—A dedicated path across the switched network.
- DLCI—The number that identifies a PVC on the switched network.
- Local Management Interface (LMI)—Provides signaling standard and status of VPNs. Also provides stats related to DLCI numbers. LMI types are CISCO, ANSI, and Q933a.

Frame Relay configuration commands:

Command	Purpose
`encapsulation frame-relay`	Interface configuration command that enables Frame Relay on an interface
`frame-relay interface-dlci [16-1007]`	Interface configuration command used to set the DLCI number for an interface or a subinterface
`frame-relay lmi-type [cisco,ansi,q933a]`	Interface configuration command that sets the LMI type for the interface
`interface s#.[subinterface number]`	Global configuration command that enables you to create subinterfaces on a Frame Relay interface

Command	Purpose
`frame-relay map [protocol] [address] [dlci #]`	Interface configuration command that enables you to map a network protocol address to the DLCI for the interface

Frame-Relay monitoring commands:

Command	Result
`show interface s#`	Provides the configuration for the interface, including Frame Relay encapsulation and DLCI number
`show frame-relay lmi`	Provides the LMI type and a list of LMI messages sent and received
`show frame-relay pvc`	Provides PVC statistics and DLCI information
`show frame-relay map`	Provides the map table for network addresses to DLCI numbers
`show frame-relay route`	Provides the input and output statistics for each DLCI
`show frame-relay traffic`	Provides statistics for the protocols running on the router related to Frame Relay traffic, such as IP

ATM (Asynchronous Transfer Mode) is a high-speed, packet-switching technology that uses a fixed size cell to move data across WANs and LANs.

ATM switches move the data through the WAN cloud and are connected to endpoint devices, such as routers, for access to LAN traffic.

ATM in the WAN environment is typically implemented over high-speed fiber optic networks, such as SONET.

A Virtual Channel (VC) is the virtual connection between a sending and receiving device on the ATM network.

Continued

A Virtual Path (VP) is a bundle or grouping of virtual channels.

ATMs use permanent virtual circuits (PVCs) as point-to-point connections between endpoints and ATM switches. A PVC is identified on the WAN by a virtual path identifier (VPI) and a virtual channel identifier (VCI). When PVCs are configured on an ATM serial interface, they must include the VPI and VCI numbers.

ATM in the LAN environment can serve as a high-speed backbone over a number of mediums, including twisted-pair wire. The LANE protocol is used by the ATM switches on the LAN to emulate two common network architectures: Ethernet and Token-Ring.

ATM router commands:

Command	Result
encapsulation atm-dxi	Interface configuration command to set ATM as the encapsulation type on a serial interface.
dxi pvc [vpi #] [vci #] [snap, nlpid, or mux]	Interface configuration command used to configure PVCs on ATM-enabled serial interfaces. The VPI and VCI are provided by the service provider. SNAP and NLPID signify that multiple protocols are running on the interface, and the PVC and MUX signifies that only one net work protocol is running on the interface.
show interfaces atm	Shows the status of ATM-enabled serial interfaces on the router.
show dxi pvc	Shows the configuration and statistics related to ATM PVCs set up on the router.

WAN Protocols—Configuring PPP and ISDN

Cisco has divided its CCNA exam objectives into nine categories. Category 1 is "Bridging/Switching" and includes PPP as an objective. PPP is an important WAN protocol, and knowledge of PPP is required for the exam. This chapter also covers another important CCNA objective—ISDN—from the "WAN Protocols" category (see the following objectives list).

- PPP
- ISDN

PPP

The Point-to-Point protocol (PPP) can be used for router-to-router connections over synchronous lines and also for host-to-network connections over asynchronous lines (a common way for connecting home computers to Internet service providers). PPP supports several LAN protocols, such as IP and IPX (additional background information on PPP can be found in the section "Point-to-Point Protocols" in Chapter 9, "WAN Protocols—HDLC Frame Relay and ATM").

Configuring PPP

To configure PPP on a serial interface, you use the encapsulation command at the configure interface prompt. Because PPP supports authentication for incoming connections to a router's serial interface, you also can set the authentication type and the username and password for the authentication of incoming calls (when a dial-up connection is used). The following figure shows the commands for enabling PPP on a router interface. The following are the steps to configuring PPP:

1. At the privileged prompt, type **config t** and press Enter. You are placed in the global configuration mode.

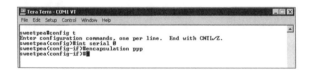

2. To configure a particular WAN interface, type the name of the interface at the prompt, such as interface serial 0. Then, press Enter. The prompt changes to the config-if mode.

3. Type **encapsulation PPP** and press Enter.

PPP supports two authentication types for authorizing incoming calls to your router: PAP and CHAP. The Password Authentication Protocol (PAP) uses a username and password in clear text format. When the remote node creates the connection, it sends a username and password. The receiving router then authenticates them. If the username and password are not accepted, the connection is terminated.

This type of password protection is referred to as a *two-way handshake.* The problem with PAP is that the clear-text username and password are susceptible to hacking—a hacker could actually capture the username and password with some sort of protocol analyzer.

The Challenge Handshake Authentication Protocol (CHAP) is a more secure authentication scheme because the username and password are not disclosed over the link as clear-text. CHAP uses a three-way handshake scheme for authentication when the remote device requests a connection. The receiving router sends a challenge message that contains a random number and asks the dialing device to send its username and password. The dialing router responds with an encrypted value that is unencrypted by the receiving device, yielding the username and password.

Enabling PAP or CHAP is accomplished at the interface configuration prompt using the ppp authentication command. For PAP, the command is ppp authentication pap; for CHAP, the command is ppp authentication chap. For two routers to connect using PPP in a dial-up situation, the receiving router must be configured with a username and password that actually refer to the username and password the router dialing in will be using for authentication. This is accomplished at the configuration prompt. The command is username [name] password [password]; where [name] is the username for the router, and [password] is the password that will be used to authenticate the username.

Viewing PPP Statistics

You can quickly check a serial connecting using PPP and view PPP statistics. To check the PPP connection between two routers, use ping [ip address command], where the IP address is the address of the target interface. On the other hand, to view the PPP settings for a particular interface, you use the show interface command. The following figure shows the results of the show interface command on a serial interface.

```
Tera Term - COM1 VT
File  Edit  Setup  Control  Window  Help

sweetpea#sh interface serial 0
Serial0 is up, line protocol is up
  Hardware is HD64570
  Internet address is 10.2.1.1/16
  MTU 1500 bytes, BW 144 Kbit, DLY 20000 usec, rely 255/255, load 1/255
  Encapsulation PPP, loopback not set, keepalive set (10 sec)
  LCP Open
  Open: IPCP, CDPCP, BRIDGECP
  Last input 00:00:09, output 00:00:01, output hang never
  Last clearing of "show interface" counters never
  Queuing strategy: fifo
  Output queue 0/40, 0 drops; input queue 0/75, 0 drops
  5 minute input rate 0 bits/sec, 0 packets/sec
  5 minute output rate 0 bits/sec, 0 packets/sec
     112544 packets input, 6106819 bytes, 0 no buffer
     Received 0 broadcasts, 0 runts, 0 giants, 0 throttles
     0 input errors, 0 CRC, 0 frame, 0 overrun, 0 ignored, 0 abort
     530280 packets output, 23851253 bytes, 0 underruns
     0 output errors, 0 collisions, 2 interface resets
     0 output buffer failures, 0 output buffers swapped out
     23 carrier transitions
     DCD=up  DSR=up  DTR=up  RTS=up  CTS=up
sweetpea#
```

ISDN

ISDN is actually a suite of protocols defined by the International Telecommunication Union-Telecommunication Standardization sector (ITU-T) that provides digital communication over existing phone lines. The CCNA exam concentrates on ISDN BRI, which is basic rate ISDN. Regarding the relevant use and context for ISDN, you should understand that ISDN provides both voice and data transmission over regular phone lines. It provides an excellent venue for telecommuters who need to connect to a corporate network remotely.

ISDN can support several data types, including voice, video, graphics, and others. ISDN is also considered a viable way to increase bandwidth for connection to the Internet (although this is being overshadowed by broadband and DSL connections, which are not covered on the CCNA exam).

ISDN implementations often take the form of dial-on-demand routing, where the ISDN connection is made on an as-needed basis. Dial-on-demand routing is not covered on the CCNA test, although ISDN use in dial-on-demand routing situations would certainly be a valid context for the use of ISDN.

ISDN comes in two formats: ISDN PRI (Primary Rate ISDN) and ISDN BRI. Both of these ISDN types are discussed in the sections that follow, with an emphasis on ISDN BRI. You will find that the various ISDN specifications relating to protocols, function groups, and ISDN channels (all important aspects of ISDN) provide you with an ample opportunity to test your ability to learn a lot of material that will probably only drill down to a handful of questions on the CCNA exam.

You are expected to know the various ITU ISDN protocols and how they map to the OSI model. You also will be tested on function groups, ISDN reference points, and the number and type of channels used on both ISDN PRI and ISDN BRI (a definite "must-know"). First, let's take a look at the ISDN protocols.

ISDN Protocols

The ISDN ITU protocols span the OSI model's Physical, Data Link, and Network layers. Several series of protocols are related to the ISDN specifications. The two most important (in respect to the CCNA test) are the I-series, which handles the ISDN concepts, structures, and interfaces; and the Q-series, which handles switching and signaling. Table 10.1 provides the mapping of the Q and I series to the appropriate OSI layer and provides a description of each of the protocols.

Table 10.1 Q and I Series Protocols

OSI Layer	ITU Protocol Specification	Description
Physical	TU-TI.430 ITU-TI.431	Handles framing and defines ISDN reference points (discussed in the next section)
Data Link	ITU-T Q.920 ITU-T Q.921	Provides specifications for the Link Access Procedure used on the D channel for signal request encapsulation (LAPD)
Network	ITU-T Q.930 ITU-T Q.931	Handles call setup and call termination messages

Understanding the function of LAPD at the Data Link layer will prepare you for the exam better than actually memorizing all the specifications in the table. LAPD delivers signaling messages to the actual ISDN switch on the D channel of ISDN BRI.

ISDN Function Groups

ISDN function groups actually refer to the terminal equipment that sits between your network and the ISDN connection. Two possibilities exist: a terminal device (your network router) with a built-in ISDN interface or a terminal device that requires an additional device to convert serial communication to ISDN signals. A description of each terminal type follows:

- **Terminal Endpoint Device-type 1 (TE1)**—A device that can handle the ISDN signaling. This would be a router with a built-in ISDN BRI interface.

- **Terminal Endpoint Device-type 2 (TE2)**—A device that does not have a built-in ISDN interface. For example, a router that does not have an ISDN interface would require an additional piece of equipment called a Terminal Adapter (TA) to make an ISDN connection to the phone system. The TA converts serial data to ISDN signals.

So, to summarize function groups: A Cisco router with a built-in ISDN interface is TE1 and ready to configure for an ISDN connection. A router or other device without a built-in ISDN interface is a TE2 and requires a TA to make the ISDN connection.

Before we end this discussion of terminal equipment, we should look at the various designations for termination devices. These devices are connected to either the TE1 or the TA (with the TA connecting to the TE2). The two network termination types are Network Termination 1 (NT1) and Network Termination 2 (NT2):

- **NT1**—A device that connects to a TE1 or TA and converts the ISDN BRI signals for use over the actual ISDN line. Typically, an NT1 is a device such as a CSU/DSU.

- **NT2**—A device that connects to a TE1 or TA and provides BRI signal conversion and ISDN concentration. A PBX is an example.

The termination devices designate the end of the customer premise network and the beginning of the ISDN local loop. In North America, the termination devices are considered customer equipment, whereas in Europe, they are provided by the carrier network.

ISDN Reference Points

After you understand the various types of devices that can be used on your end of the ISDN connection—a TE1 (router with ISDN interface) or a TE2 (router or other terminal device without an ISDN Interface) attached to a TA—and the types of termination devices (NT1 and NT2), you can then map out the various reference points used to describe the logical connections or interfaces between these devices. Table 10.2 provides a summary of the ISDN reference points, and the following figure provides a diagram of the reference point types.

Table 10.2 Summary of the ISDN Reference Points

Reference Point Designation	Definition
R	Reference point between non-ISDN terminal equipment, TE2, (such as a router), and a TA
S	Reference point between a TE1 and a NT2 device
T	Reference point between an NT1 (such as a CSU/DSU) and an NT2 (such as a PBX)
U	Reference point between an NT1 and the line-termination equipment provided by the service provider

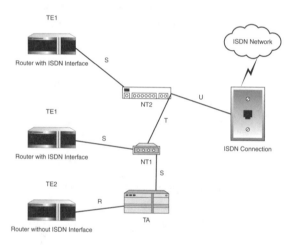

ISDN Channels

As already mentioned, ISDN comes in two formats: ISDN BRI (Basic Rate Interface) and ISDN PRI (Primary Rate Interface). BRI consists of two data channels designated as B channels. Each B channel provides a throughput of 64Kbps. A D channel of 16Kbps is also provided for link management. The two BRI channels can be combined for data throughput of 128Kbps.

PRI consists of 23 64Kbps B channels and 1 64Kbps D channel. ISDN PRI uses 24 channels total, which is the equivalent of 1 T1 communication line.

For the exam, remember that the B channels are used to move data and the D channel is used to convey control information between sending and receiving devices.

Cisco's Implementation of ISDN BRI

The CCNA exam concentrates on ISDN BRI and how you configure it on a router. As mentioned previously, ISDN BRI consists of two B carrier channels and one D channel carrying control and signaling information.

ISDN BRI is typically implemented in dial-on-demand routing situations in which data is moved at certain times after the BRI connection is made as opposed to a constant connection providing constant data flow.

ISDN BRI is typically configured on a router that has a built-in BRI interface. To configure BRI, you must select the switch type to which your BRI is connected and select an encapsulation type, such as PPP or HDLC. Here's a tip related to a probable exam question: For dial-on-demand ISDN BRI connections, remember that you must use PPP if you want to take advantage of PAP or CHAP authentication for the connection.

Other information that must be provided are SPID numbers. A *SPID (service profile identifier)* identifies each B channel. The SPID number also authenticates the channel to the switch that connects the ISDN-enabled route to the phone system. Each channel must have a different SPID number. Follow these steps:

1. At the privileged prompt, type **config t** and press Enter. You are placed in the global configuration mode.

2. To set the switch type for your ISDN connection, type **isdn switch-type basic-[switch identifier]**, where the switch identifier is the manufacturer ID code for the switch type to which you will connect. Press Enter.

3. Now, you can configure the ISDN interface. Type **int bri [number]**, where [number] is the BRI interface number on the router, such as BRI 0 or BRI 1. Press Enter.

4. At the config-if prompt, enter the encapsulation type (such as encap ppp), and then press Enter.

5. To provide the SPID number for the two ISDN B channels at the config-if prompt, type **isdn spid1 [SPID #]**, where [SPID #] is the telephone number provided by your service provider to reach the particular channel. Press Enter.

6. To provide the SPID number for the second channel, repeat the isdn spid2 [SPID #] command using the SPID number for the second channel. Press Enter after typing the command at the config-if prompt.

7. When you have completed entering the information outlined in the previous steps, press Ctrl+Z to end the configuration session.

The following figure shows the configuration command sequence for enabling the ISDN BRI on a Cisco router.

TAKE THE TEST

This Practice Test provides you with questions related to the PPP objective found in the CCNA "Bridging/Switching" category and the ISDN objective found in the "WAN Protocols" category. Because the CCNA exam is in a multiple-choice format, these questions are formatted as they would be on the actual exam.

1. To used PPP as the encapsulation type for a serial interface, the command sequence at the configuration prompt is

   A. `interface E0, encapsulation PPP`

   B. `encapsulation ppp`

   C. `int s0, encap ppp`

   D. `show interface serial 0`

Answer A is incorrect; PPP can serve only as the encapsulation type on a serial interface, not a LAN interface such as Ethernet 0. Answer B is incorrect; a serial interface must be designated at the configuration prompt before the encapsulation command can be used. **Answer C is correct; a serial interface has been designated and `encap ppp` is a valid abbreviation for enabling PPP encapsulation on a serial interface.** Answer D is incorrect; the `show interface serial 0` command shows only statistics for a route interface, such as the encapsulation type; it does not enable you to specify configuration parameters.

2. PAP is a more secure authentication scheme for PPP connections when compared to CHAP.

   A. True

   B. False

Answer A is incorrect; PAP is not a more secure authentication method than CHAP. PAP actually sends the password in clear-text format, providing the opportunity for the password to be read by someone with a network analyzer. **Answer B is correct; CHAP is a more secure authentication scheme than PAP. CHAP uses challenge messages and encryption to provide secure authentication.**

   3. To view PPP activity on a serial interface use the command:

    A. `show ppp`

    B. `ping`

    C. `show interface serial [interface number]`

    D. `show running-configuration`

Answer A is incorrect; no command is available that enables you to directly list PPP parameters without specifying an interface. Answer B is incorrect; `ping` is used to test a serial connection between two routers but provides no encapsulation information. **Answer C is correct; the `show interface` command provides specific encapsulation information and PPP statistics for a serial interface configured for PPP.** Answer D is incorrect; the `show running-configuration` command does not provide specific information for the router interfaces and their encapsulation protocol.

   4. Which ISDN series of protocols handles switching and signaling standards?

    A. I Series

    B. Q Series

    C. TU-TI.430

    D. LAPD

Answer A is incorrect; the I series of protocols handles ISDN concepts, structures, and interfaces. **Answer B is correct; the Q series of ISDN protocols is responsible for switching and signaling.** Answer C is incorrect; TU-TI.430 is an I series protocol, which does not handle ISDN switching and signaling. Answer D is incorrect; LAPD is not a series of ISDN protocol but rather one of the specific Q series protocols.

5. A router with a built-in ISDN interface would be considered which type of function group?

  A. TA

  B. TE2

  C. TE1

  D. ISDN BRI

Answer A is incorrect; a TA is required for a TE2 device that does not have a built-in ISDN interface. Answer B is incorrect; a TE2 does not have a built-in ISDN interface and so requires a TA to connect to an ISDN line. **Answer C is correct; TE2 terminal devices have a built-in ISDN interface.** Answer D is incorrect; ISDN BRI is a type of ISDN.

6. What is the reference point for a connection between a TE1 and an NT2 device?

  A. R

  B. S

  C. T

  D. U

Answer A is incorrect; reference point R defines the connection between a TE2 and a TA. **Answer B is correct; reference point S is the reference point between a TE1 and an NT2 device.** Answer C is incorrect; the T reference point defines the connections between an NT1 and an NT2. Answer D is incorrect; the U reference point defines the connection between an NT1 and line termination equipment.

7. What is the Kbps for a single ISDN B channel?

  A. 128

  B. 16

  C. 64

  D. 2

Answer A is incorrect; this is the Kbps that can be attained by combining the two B channels on an ISDN BRI interface. Answer B is incorrect; 16Kbps is the D channel throughput on an ISDN BRI connection. **Answer C is correct; ISDN D channels have a throughput of 64Kbps.** Answer D is incorrect; it specifies the number of B channels on an ISDN BRI.

8. Which three parameters must be set to enable a router's ISDN BRI interface?

   A. ISDN switch type

   B. Encapsulation type

   C. ISDN reference points

   D. SPID numbers

Answer A is correct; the type of service provider switch to which the ISDN BRI interface will be connected must be specified. Answer B is correct; an encapsulation type, such as PPP, must be specified for the ISDN BRI interface. Answer C is incorrect; ISDN reference points provide logical mapping between network devices but are not configured on the router. **Answer D is correct; the SPID number for each ISDN BRI B channel must be configured.**

Cheat Sheet

The Point-to-Point protocol (PPP) can be used for router-to-router connections over synchronous lines and also for host-to-network connections over asynchronous lines.

PPP is enabled at the interface configuration prompt using the `encapsulation PPP` command.

PPP connections can be authenticated with PAP or CHAP. PAP uses clear-text transfer of username and password, making PAP authentication susceptible to hacking. CHAP provides a three-way handshake with encryption for greater security.

ISDN protocols consist of the I and Q series, which span the OSI Physical, Data Link, and Network layers. The I series handles concepts structures and interfaces, and the Q-series handles switching and signaling.

LAPD is a Q-series ISDN protocol responsible for D channel signal request encapsulation.

ISDN function groups, termination devices, and reference points:

Item	Description
TE1	A device that can handle the ISDN signaling
TE2	A device that cannot handle the ISDN signaling and requires a TA
TA	A device that enables a terminal device, such as a router, without an ISDN interface for ISDN
NT1	A device that connects to a TE1 or TA and then to the ISDN line
NT2	A device that connects to a TE1 or TA and provides concentration and connection to the ISDN line
R	Reference point between non-ISDN terminal equipment, TE2 (such as a router), and a TA
S	Reference point between a TE1 and an NT2 device
T	Reference point between an NT1 (such as a CSU/DSU) and an NT2 (such as a PBX)
U	Reference point between an NT1 and the line-termination equipment provided by the service provider

Continued

ISDN interfaces have two types of channels: B channels and D channels.

ISDN BRI consists of two 64Kbps B channels and one 16Kbps D channel.

ISDN PRI consists of 23 64Kbps B channels and 1 64Kbps D channel.

ISDN BRI is used for dial-on-demand routing between Cisco routers.

ISDN is configured using the following commands:

```
isdn switch-type basic-[switch identifier]
```

This is a global configuration command used to set the service provider switch type.

```
encapsulation [protocol]
```

This interface configuration command is used to set the ISDN BRI encapsulation type.

```
isdn spid[1 or 2][spid #]
```

This interface configuration command for ISDN BRI is used to set the SPID number for the two B channels on the interface.

Access Lists and Network Troubleshooting

Cisco has divided its CCNA exam objectives into nine categories. Category 6 is "Network Management," and this chapter covers the Access Lists objective from this category. Access lists in both the TCP/IP and Novell NetWare environments are covered. Category 9, "Cisco Basics, IOS, and Network Basics" includes the Troubleshooting objective, which is also covered in this chapter (see the following objective list).

- Access Lists
- Troubleshooting

Access Lists

Access lists are a list of conditions called `permit` and `deny` statements that help regulate traffic flow into and out of a router. A `permit` statement basically means that packets meeting a certain conditional statement will not be filtered (they are "permitted" to continue their journey across the interface), and a `deny` statement specifies the packets to be filtered (filtered means discarded).

Access lists can be used to deny the flow of packets into a particular router interface or out of a particular router interface. Access lists are not only used to filter packet traffic, but they can also be used as a security measure because they can deny access to a router interface by blocking packets originating from a particular Application layer protocol (such as extended IP access lists).

Access lists take the form of several `permit` and `deny` statements, and each packet entering the interface is compared to each line in the access list in sequential order. When a match is made (based on addressing or protocol criteria) between the packet and a line in the access list, the router acts on the packet (either permitting or denying access to it). No further action is taken on the packet. An implicit `deny` statement is created at the end of each access list to deny packets that do not meet any of the criteria in the access list. This implicit `deny` statement means that your access list must provide permit statements for any and all traffic that will be allowed to access a particular interface on the router (the interface that has the access list applied to it). You must keep this in mind if your access lists are to work correctly.

To use an access list in association with a particular router interface, you must first create the access list itself. Then, the access list can be applied to the interface.

Access lists can be created for any routed network protocol, such as TCP/IP and IPX/SPX (both of which are discussed in this chapter). In the case of IP access lists, *standard* IP access lists and *extended* IP access lists exist. These two types of IP access lists are discussed in the two sections that follow.

Standard IP Access Lists

Standard IP access lists are configured on the router by specifying the access list with a number that ranges from 1–99. Standard IP access lists filter traffic based on the source IP address. So, the `permit` and `deny` statements in the access list denote source IP addresses. However, because you will typically want to filter traffic based on subnets or networks (rather than individual IP addresses), a wildcard mask is usually employed to accompany the IP addresses in a `permit` or `deny` statement.

A wildcard mask is a 4-octet, 32-bit mask used to denote the bits in an IP address that should be paid attention to when the address is compared to statements in the access list. A way to denote bits that should be ignored when the address is compared to the list is also required.

For example, suppose we have a Class C major network address—200.90.20.0—where we want all the bits in the first, second, and third octets to be checked by the router when it works through the statements in the access list. The wildcard mask would be 0.0.0.255 (the binary equivalent of these decimal values would be 00000000 00000000 00000000 11111111).

The wildcard mask denotes that all the bits in the first, second, and third octets of the packets should be checked; a 0 in the mask means that the bit should be compared to the address bit in the access list statement. A 1 in the mask means that the bit in the address should be ignored. In the previous statement, the last octet should be ignored; again, because a one bit in the mask tells the router to ignore that particular bit in a packet's address.

Using the IP address and the wildcard mask in our example, the `access-list` statement would look similar to the following (entered at the router's configuration prompt):

```
access-list [1-99] [permit or deny] 200.90.20.0 0.0.255
```

Because the access list is a standard IP access list, it is specified with a number from 1–99, either `permit` or `deny` is entered in the statement, and then it's followed by the source IP address and the wildcard mask.

As you can see, working with access list statements that specify all the packets from a particular IP network is fairly simple because you use a wildcard mask that consists of only 0s and 1s (denoted by either the decimal 0 or the decimal 255).

Complex IP Wildcard Masks

access-list statements can become confusing when you want to use the wildcard mask and an IP address to denote a range of IP addresses. For example, let's say you want to deny an entire subnet of addresses—from 130.10.32.0 to 130.10.63.0—using a deny access list statement. This statement would read deny 130.10.32.0 0.0.15.255. The IP address of the first subnet follows the deny statement, and the wildcard mask follows the IP address. The big question is, how did we come up with the wildcard mask?

For packets to be acted on by the deny statement in the access list, their first octet must match the decimal value 130. Therefore, the wildcard mask for that octet in binary will be 00000000—0 in decimal. This means all the bits in the first octet of the packet must match the binary value of 130 (10000010), and the second octet must match the binary equivalent of 10 (00001010). So, again, its wildcard mask will be 00000000 (0 in decimal), which means that so far our wildcard mask is 0.0.

Now things get complicated because we are at the third octet, where bits have been borrowed for subnetting. We must ensure the first, second, and third bits in the octet are checked (this is the 128, 64, and 32 bits). This means that the first three binary values in our wildcard mask will be 000.

As for the rest of the bits in the third octet of an address being compared to the access list statement, we don't care what those values are. So, the last five bits in the wildcard mask would be set to 1, which means ignore these bits when comparing an IP address to our access-list statement.

This means that our wildcard mask from left to right for the third octet will read 00011111 because we want the router to compare the first, second, and third bits of incoming packets to the IP address that appears in the access-list statement. To compute the decimal value of this wildcard mask, we add the values of the bits in the mask that are set to 1: 16+8+4+2+1=31. Therefore, our wildcard mask for our access list deny statement will read 0.0.31 for the first three octets in the wildcard mask.

Because we are not concerned with the information related to the node addresses in the last octet of the IP addresses of packets processed by our access list, the last octet wildcard value will be set to all 1s (11111111). This makes the decimal value of the last octet in our wildcard mask 255. Our complete wildcard mask to filter out (deny) packets from the subnet range 130.10.32.0–130.10.63.0 will be 0.0.31.255.

Configuring and Grouping Standard IP Access Lists

Standard IP access lists are created in the configuration mode one statement at a time. After the list has been created, the list must then be grouped to a particular interface on the router. The list can be grouped to the interface and filter packets either coming into that interface or leaving that interface.

Filtering packets entering an interface using access lists serves as a good security measure (keeping bad traffic out, such as a hacker's probes). Filtering packets leaving an interface enables you to decide which packets can take a particular route from an interface, such as an interface connected to a dial-on-demand ISDN line that should carry only packets from specific users on the network. This basically keeps a higher-cost WAN connection free for only important traffic (such as data moving from a branch bank to the main office). Follow these steps:

1. At the privileged prompt, type **config t** and press Enter. You are placed in the global configuration mode.

2. To create the first line in the access list, type **access-list [list #] permit or deny [ip address] wildcard mask**; where [list #] is a number from 1–99. The statement can contain only deny or permit (not both).

3. Repeat step 2 with any additional permit or deny statements you want to have in the access list. The following figure shows the configuration of a standard IP access list.

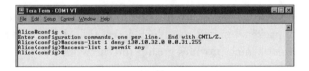

In cases where you want to permit or deny all IP addresses not specified in the access list with the use of specific IP addresses and wildcard masks, you can use the statement [permit or deny] any. The figure uses the statement to permit any packets other than those specified in the access list. This is important because an implicit deny any statement is placed at the end of your access list when you create it.

After you've configured your access list, you must apply it to a particular interface. The command used at the interface configuration prompt is ip access-group [access list #] [in or out], where the access list number is the number you assigned to the access list when you created it. You must also determine whether you want to filter packets entering the interface (in) or leaving the interface (out). The following figure shows the grouping of an IP access list to an Ethernet interface on a router.

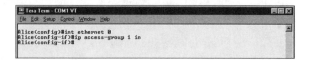

After the access list has been applied to the interface, the filtering of packets will begin using the access list as the test list for the acceptance or denial of packets. Remember that only one standard IP access list can be applied to an interface for incoming packets (in) and one for outgoing packets (out).

Extended IP Access Lists

Although the CCNA exam concentrates on access list concepts and basic IP access lists, you also must know how extended IP access lists work and are configured. Extended IP access lists give you greater flexibility in filtering packets. Packets can be filtered by a source address as found in standard IP access lists, but other parameters can also be used for the filtering process. Packets can be filtered by the destination address of the packet, the Transport layer protocol header of the packet (TCP or UDP), and the Application layer protocol header port number (for example, a port number such as 23, which is the port number associated with Telnet).

With more possibilities for precise filtering of packets, router interfaces not only filter data packets but can also block access to interfaces on routers (such as Telnet sessions), which provides greater internetwork security.

To use extended IP access lists, specifically those that filter by protocol and port numbers, you must know the well-known port numbers for the various TCP/IP Application layer protocols and the Transport layer protocol that serves them (TCP or UDP).

Table 11.1 provides a list of some of the TCP/IP Application layer protocols, their port numbers, and the Transport layer protocol they use.

Table 11.1 Port Numbers and Their Associated Transport Protocols

Protocol	Port Number	Transport Protocol
HTTP	80	UDP
FTP	21	TCP
TFTP	69	UDP
SMTP	25	TCP
SNMP	161	UDP
DNS	53	UDP
Telnet	23	TCP

Extended IP access lists take pretty much the same format as standard IP access lists. A deny or permit statement that expresses parameters that should be used for the filtering of packets is created in the configuration mode; the access list is then grouped to a particular router interface to filter either incoming or outgoing packets. The next section discusses how access list statements are designed for extended IP access lists that filter by more than just the IP source address.

Configuring Extended IP Access Lists

Configuring extended IP access lists requires that you include additional information in your access list deny or permit statements, which are then used by the router to either pass on or filter packets meeting your statement's criteria. This information (as already mentioned) relates to the destination address of the packet and protocol header and socket information.

Extended IP access lists are designated using the numbers 100–199. The actual extended access list configuration command takes the following format:

```
access-list [100-199] [permit or deny] [TCP/IP protocol] [source
address]
[source wildcard mask] [destination address] [destination wildcard
mask]
[eq port number]
```

The access list number and the permit or deny parameter is straightforward, but let's break down the various other parameters:

- **TCP/IP protocol**—The protocol header by which you want to filter, such as IP, TCP, UDP, or ICMP

215

- **source address**—The source of the packet
- **source wildcard mask**—The wildcard mask used with the source address provided
- **destination address**—The destination of the packet
- **destination wildcard mask**—The wildcard mask used in conjunction with the destination address
- **eq port number**—eq followed by an actual port number that specifies the upper-layer protocol port number (and relates back to the TCP/IP protocol specified, such as TCP or UDP)

Let's take a look at an actual extended IP access list statement:

```
access-list 100 deny tcp 129.5.0.0 0.0.255.255 host 10.1.1.1
eq 23
```

This access list statement denies any packets with a network source address of 129.5.0.0.0 that have a TCP header and a destination port of 23 (which is Telnet). Notice that the destination address is not followed by a wildcard mask but is preceded by the word host. The word host before an IP address in an access list is the same as using the 0.0.0.0 wildcard mask, which means that the packet address must completely match the destination address in the list statement.

The final part of the statement, eq 23, refers to the port number that should be blocked on the destination interface. The eq means match the port number that follows, which in this case is 23. Port 23 is Telnet, so this access list blocks Telnet attempts to the destination IP address 10.1.1.1, which could be the IP address of an interface on your router.

In the case of port numbers, several operators can be used to specify that there should be a direct match of a particular port number or a range of port numbers. These operators are as follows:

- **eq**—Matches the given port number only; an abbreviation for equal
- **lt**—Matches port numbers lower than the port number specified; an abbreviation for less than
- **gt**—Matches port numbers higher than the port number specified; an abbreviation for greater than
- **range**—Enables you to specify a range of port numbers that should be matched

OK, let's take a look at another example:

```
access-list 101 deny udp any 130.1.0.0 0.0.255.255 eq 69
```

In this example, TFTP (port 69) packets (which use UDP transport) are denied from any network when sent to any addresses in the 130.1.0.0 network. The any statement implies a source address with a wildcard mask of 255.255.255.255. This means that any source address will be denied.

Notice that both examples were deny statements—IP extended access lists are used to shore up internetwork security.

An extended IP access list is configured at the configuration prompt one line at a time. The following figure shows the command syntax for our first access list example.

After you have created an extended IP access list, you must group it to a particular router interface (just as you would a standard IP access list). This is accomplished using the ip access-group [access list #] [in or out] command at the interface configuration prompt.

Monitoring IP Access Lists

You also must know the commands that enable you to view access lists that have been created on the router and information relating to the interfaces to which an access list has been grouped. The most useful access list viewing and monitoring commands are as follows:

- **show access-lists**—This show command provides a list of all access lists configured on the router (including IPX, AppleTalk, or any other LAN protocol access lists created). The following figure shows the results of this command.

- **show ip access-lists**—This show command provides a list of only the IP access lists.

- **show ip interface**—This show command provides a listing of IP-enabled interfaces on the router and any access lists that have been grouped to specific interfaces. The following figure shows IP access list 1 grouped to an ISDN BRI interface.

- **show running-config**—This show command provides a listing of the running configuration, including access lists grouped to various router interfaces.

IPX Access Lists and SAP Filters

IPX standard access lists are similar to IP standard access lists with the exception that IPX standard lists filter packets based on both source and destination IPX addresses. IPX access lists also do not use wildcard masks, so you can filter using either a particular IPX network address or a host address.

IPX extended access lists also filter based on source and destination address, but they also provide additional filtering capabilities based on IPX protocol, such as SAP, SPX, NCP, and NetBIOS. In addition, IPX extended access lists can filter based on IPX socket.

IPX access lists can be viewed using commands similar to those used for IP access lists. For example, the show ipx access-lists command lists all IPX lists on the router. show ipx interfaces lists IPX-enabled interfaces and any access lists associated with them.

For the CCNA exam, you should be sure you understand the basic structure of IPX standard and extended access lists and know how to use IPX SAP filters. SAP filters are not a type of extended IPX access; they're a separate type of access list that enables you to filter SAP broadcasts from NetWare servers and IPX-enabled routers. IPX standard access lists, IPX extended access lists, and SAP filters are discussed in the next three sections, respectively.

IPX Standard Access Lists

IPX standard access lists are numbered 800–899. The access list is created one line at a time and then grouped to a particular IPX interface on the router. The configuration prompt command to create an IPX standard access list takes the following form:

```
access list [800-899] permit or deny [source] [destination]
```

The source address is the network or node address of the packet source, and the destination address is the network or node address to which the packets are being sent. In IPX access lists, the value –1 can be used as a wildcard that refers to all IPX networks and is useful in permit and deny all statements (referring to all networks not listed in more specific deny and permit statements).

As with other access lists, an IPX standard list must first be created and then grouped to a router interface. The following figure shows a standard access list that contains two statements. The first statement denies packets from network 763B20F3 that are being sent to network 02B2F4. The second statement uses the –1 wildcard and permits packets from all other IPX networks to all other IPX networks. The access list is then grouped to IPX interface Ethernet 0.

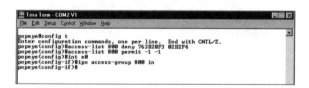

Because an implicit deny all statement is placed at the bottom of standard IPX lists, you might wonder why you would use deny statements in your access lists at all. It depends on your approach to access lists. You can assume that everything is denied by the deny all statement and then create permit statements that allow packets from particular networks to be sent to the network attached to the interface. On a large internetwork, however, this can result in a very large access list (a large number of permit statements, that is).

Another approach, as shown in our example, is that you can use permit statements (even a permit all statement) that allow large chunks of the network

219

traffic (from the various segments) and then use individual deny statements to "disallow" certain traffic.

So, whether you approach access lists from the perspective that you would rather use individual permit statements to allow traffic (falling back on the deny all statement for security), or open the floodgates with several broad-based permit statements and then whittle the traffic down using individual deny statements is really a matter of personal preference. Just keep in mind that for manageability's sake, you should try to create your access lists to perform their intended functions with the fewest number of statements possible.

IPX Extended Access Lists

IPX extended access lists are numbered using the range 900–999. You do not need to understand all the finer details related to IPX extended access lists, such as the various socket numbers used by the different protocols on a NetWare server (such as NCP, RIP, SPX, and so on). For the CCNA exam, though, you should know the general format for creating an IPX extended access list.

The configuration command for an IPX extended access list is

```
access-list [900-999] permit or deny [protocol name] [source
address] [socket]
[destination address] [socket]
```

After you create an extended access list, you group it to an IPX interface just as you would an IPX standard list. Use the command

```
ipx access-group [access-list number] in or out
```

A downside of IPX extended access lists is the use of sockets as a filtering mechanism. IPX sockets are not the same as the well-known port number used in IP filtering, but they can actually be dynamically assigned by a client or server. Therefore, the socket number does not always refer to the same resource in all cases.

SAP Filters

SAP (Service Advertisement Protocol) advertises the availability of various resources on the NetWare network. NetWare servers broadcast SAP packets every 60 seconds to let client machines on the network know where file and print services can be accessed. SAP broadcasts can lead to a great deal of traffic on the internetwork, so filtering SAP broadcasts using SAP filters can help protect network bandwidth.

IPX SAP filters are assigned the access list numbers 1000–1099. The format for the configuration command that enables you to create a SAP filter is as follows:

```
access-list [1000-1099] permit or deny [source address] [service type]
```

The source address is the network or node address from which you want to block SAP broadcasts, and the service type is the SAP number for the type of server from which you are blocking the broadcasts.

Some common SAP numbers (designating service type) appear in Table 11.2.

Table 11.2   SAP Service Types

Service Type	SAP Number
NetWare file server	4
Advertising print server	47
NetWare directory server	278
NetWare access server	98
Wildcard (specifies all services)	0

If you want to create a SAP filter that will block printer server announcements from a print server with the address 763B20F3.1234, your configuration command would look like the following:

```
access-list 1000 deny 763B20F3.1234 47
```

After you create the list, you can then assign it to a particular IPX interface on the router. The command syntax is different from the command used to group other access list types to interfaces.

You can apply your SAP filter to an interface so that it works as either an input filter or an output filter. As an input filter, the SAP filter prevents SAP broadcast information from being added to the router's SAP table. As an output filter, it keeps the router from advertising its SAP table out of the particular interface.

To apply a SAP filter as an input filter, first specify the router interface in the configuration mode. Then, use the following command:

```
ipx input-sap-filter [access-list number]
```

221

The access list number is the number you assigned your SAP filter when you created it. To apply a SAP filter as an out filter, again, you must be in the interface configuration mode and then use the following command:

```
ipx output-sap-filter [access-list number]
```

As far as the CCNA exam goes, you should concentrate on IPX standard access lists and SAP broadcasts. At most, a fairly small pool of questions will be directed at IPX access lists in general.

Troubleshooting

Even though troubleshooting internetworks and internetworking devices such as routers is certainly not emphasized on the CCNA exam, you should know some basics related to troubleshooting. (A separate Internetworking Troubleshooting exam exists for the Cisco Certified Network Professional certification.)

The following is something that really can't be tested on a multiple-choice exam, but I feel I should mention it anyway. A great deal of problems related to internetworks and networks in general are related to physical connections. For example, bad cabling, a bad hub, and a bad controller card on a router interface all can lead to major network and routing problems. In terms of what you might be tested on, you should know the syntax of the `show interface` command, which enables you to check the status of various router interface types. You also should know how to check connectivity over the internetwork using commands such as `ping` and `trace`. First, we'll discuss the `show interface` command on various interface types and then take a look at `ping` and `trace`.

The `show interfaces ethernet` Command

We've already taken a look at the `show` command in Chapter 3, "The Cisco IOS—Basic Router Commands." As far as troubleshooting is concerned, the `show interface` command is particularly useful.

For example, suppose you have a problem with an Ethernet subnet on your network. Because Ethernet is a passive network architecture that uses Carrier Sense Multiple Access with Collision Detection (CSMA/CD) as its strategy for network access, problems related to Ethernet can revolve around excess collisions on the network. This can be due to cable breaks, cable runs that exceed the maximum length allowed, or malfunctioning network cards that can cause excessive broadcast traffic.

The `show interfaces ethernet [interface number]` command enables you to view statistics related to a particular Ethernet interface and determine whether it is experiencing an excessive amount of collisions. The following figure shows the results of this command on an Ethernet 0 interface.

Being able to troubleshoot the network based on the various statistics provided by this command requires that you know what each statistic is telling you:

- **Ethernet 0 is Up, Line Protocol is up**—This lets you know that the interface is active and that the Ethernet protocols believe the line is usable. If the interface is down, check the LAN connection to the interface. You can also enter the interface configuration mode and "bounce" the interface, which means you shut it off and then turn it back on. Use the `shut` command (to down the interface), and then use the `no shut` command to bring up the interface. This can bring the interface back up.

- **Hardware Address**—This is the hexadecimal MAC address for the interface.

- **Internet Address**—This is the IP address and subnet mask assigned to the interface.

- **MTU**—This is the maximum transmission unit for the interface in bytes.

- **BW**—This is the bandwidth for the interface in kilobits/second.

- **Rely**—This is a measurement of the reliability of the line, with 255/255 being 100% reliable. The lower the first number in the reliability measurement, the less reliable the interface connection (due to downed lines or other problems).

- **Load**—This measures the current load on the interface. The measurement 255/255 is a completely saturated interface (meaning too much traffic; you might need to add another interface or router to service the network LAN).

- **Encapsulation**—This is the Ethernet frame type assigned to the interface. ARPA is the default and is the 802.2 Ethernet frame type. If the frame type does not match the frame type used on your network (such as an older NetWare network using 802.3 raw frames), you must reset the frame type. Use the `arp` command at the config-if prompt for the interface and assign the correct Ethernet encapsulation type (such as arpa or snap).

- **Collisions**—This shows the number of collisions monitored by the interface. A large number of collisions means that some physical problem might exist on the network, such as a break in a cable or a malfunctioning network interface card that is generating a large amount of broadcast traffic. This could also mean that cables are too long on the LAN.

Notice that this one command not only gives you information related to the configuration of the interface, such as the IP address, but also provides information on the general health of the LAN to which the interface is connected, such as the number of collisions on the subnet.

The `show interfaces tokenring` Command

The `show interface` command also can be used to check the status and configuration of Token-Ring interfaces. The command syntax is `show interfaces tokenring [interface number]`. The following figure shows the results of this command on a router's Token-Ring interface.

Token-Ring is de-emphasized on the exam in favor of Ethernet; however, remember that problems related to Token-Ring networks, such as unbalanced rings, and interface problems can be diagnosed using the show interfaces tokenring [interface number] command. What the results of show interfaces tokenring command are telling you is detailed in the list that follows:

- **Token Ring is Up (or down)**—This lets you know that the interface is currently active. If the interface is down, you can try to bounce the interface in the configuration-if mode to get it back online.

- **Hardware Address**—This is the hexadecimal MAC address for the interface.

- **Internet Address**—This is the IP address and subnet mask assigned to the interface.

- **MTU**—This is the maximum transmission unit for the interface in bytes.

- **BW**—This is the bandwidth for the interface in kilobits/second.

- **Rely**—This is a measurement of the reliability of the line, with 255/255 being 100% reliable. This measurement is averaged for the interface over a period of five minutes.

- **Load**—This measures the current load on the interface. The measurement 255/255 is a completely saturated interface and again means that you might have a Token-Ring LAN that's too large being serviced by the one interface on the router.

- **Ring Speed**—This is setting for the speed of the Token-Ring LAN to which the router is connected. All devices on the Token-Ring network, including the router, must be using the same ring speed (either 4Mbps or 16Mbps). Any mismatches will result in an interruption in the flow of data. To check the ring speed set on the router, use the show running-config command. If you need to reset the ring speed, enter the config-if mode on the router console for the interface. Then, use the ring-speed command to reset the ring speed.

- **Restarts**—On Token-Ring interfaces, this value should always be 0. If it is any number other than 0, the interface has been restarted because of some problem on the Token-Ring LAN.

As far as troubleshooting Token-Ring and the CCNA exam are concerned, you could face a question related to mismatched ring speeds. Remember the show interface tokenring command enables you to diagnose this problem.

The show interface serial Command

The show interface command is also useful in troubleshooting problems associated with serial interfaces. However, troubleshooting serial interfaces is trickier because of the wide variety of encapsulation types available (everything from HDLC to PPP to Frame Relay). And, sometimes problems arise because of the service provider's leased lines or packet-switching network, which provides you with little alternative other than waiting for the line to come up or having a redundant connection on the router through which you can route the packets.

The following figure shows the results of the show interface serial 0 command. A list follows the figure that defines the various statistics provided by the command.

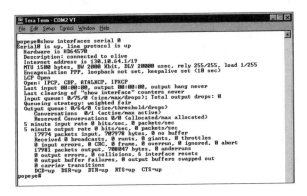

- **Serial 0 is up**—This lets you know that the interface is active. If the interface is down, a problem could exist with the connection from the router to the CSU/DSU or with the telephone line that connects the CSU/DSU to the WAN.

- **Line Protocol is up**—This lets you know that the WAN protocols in use believe the line is usable. If the line protocol is down, your router might not be configured correctly (use the show running-config command to check this).

- **Internet Address**—This is the IP address and subnet mask assigned to the interface.

- **MTU**—This is the maximum transmission unit for the interface in bytes.

- **BW**—This is the bandwidth for the interface in kilobits/second. This is set for the interface at the config-if prompt using the bandwidth command. The bandwidth must be set to a value that coincides with the speed of the line to which the router's serial interface is connected.

- **Rely**—This is a measurement of the reliability of the line, with 255/255 being 100% reliable. The lower the first number in the reliability measurement, the less reliable the interface connection (due to downed lines or other problems).

- **Load**—This measures the current load on the interface. The measurement 255/255 is a completely saturated interface (meaning too much traffic; you might need to add another interface or router to service the LAN).

- **Encapsulation**—This is the WAN protocol assigned to the interface. It must match the WAN protocol on the router at the other end of the connection. The WAN protocol must also be set for the type of service you are being provided from your service provider (don't set it for PPP if you are connecting to a Frame Relay switch).

- **CRC**—This shows the number of cyclical redundancy checks that have failed on incoming packets. This is usually an indication that the line provided by the phone company is experiencing a great deal of noise or that your serial cable from the router to the CSU/DSU is too long.

Be sure that you get some router time so you can run the various show interface commands (such as the show int serial command discussed in this section). Taking the time to see the type of results these commands provide on a router that is actually handling data traffic will help you understand the troubleshooting questions you face on the exam.

Checking Network Connections

In Chapter 6, "Network Protocols—TCP/IP," we discussed the ping and trace commands and how they use ICMP packets to check the connection between two devices or trace the route between two devices, respectively. ping and trace also prove to be two of the handiest troubleshooting commands on the router related to internetworking connectivity. For the exam, know how both can be used.

ping provides a quick way to check the connection between two nodes on a network or an internetwork. For example, you can use it to check the connection between two routers using LAN or WAN connections.

To use ping on an IP network, type **ping [ip address]**, where you supply the IP address of the destination router interface or node on the network. Another form of the ping command, extended ping, also can be used to check connectivity on IPX networks.

To use the extended ping command, type **ping** at the router prompt and press Enter. You are then asked to specify the protocol, such as IP or IPX, and then supply the address of the remote node (such as the IP address or IPX network and node address). Other parameters, such as the size of the ping packet and the timeout (in seconds), also can be set.

ping can only tell you whether you are connected to a remote node or not connected. It provides no other information. When ping times out because it gets no response from the remote node, the cause is either a physical connection problem or an incorrectly configured device.

trace is another command that can be used to troubleshoot connectivity problems on an IP internetwork. It enables you to see the route the packets take from source to destination. This enables you to determine whether routers that would normally participate in the path between a particular router and node or router and router are currently down. To use the trace command, type **trace [ip address]**, where you specify the IP address of the remote device.

trace is also useful in determining whether certain routes (and therefore router interfaces) are down on the internetwork. If a particular router is not listed in the results of trace, you know that the router is down or the router's interface is having problems.

TAKE THE TEST

This Practice Test provides you with questions related to the Access Lists objective found in the CCNA "Network Management" category and the Troubleshooting objective found in the "Cisco Basics, IOS, and Network Basics" category. Because the CCNA exam is in a multiple-choice format, these questions are formatted as they would be on the actual exam.

1. IP standard access lists can filter packets based on

   A. Destination IP address

   B. Port number

   C. Source address

   D. Protocol

Answer A is incorrect; IP extended access lists can use destination addresses, not standard access lists. Answer B is incorrect; port numbers can be used by only IP extended access lists for filtering. **Answer C is correct; source addresses are used for filtering by standard IP access lists.** Answer D is incorrect; standard IP access lists cannot filter by protocol as can IP extended access lists.

2. The standard IP access list command access list 1 deny 130.10.0.0 0.0.255.255 would filter packets with the following addresses (select all that apply):

   A. 130.10.1.1

   B. 130.11.1.1

   C. 130.10.40.1

   D. 10.0.0.0

Answer A is correct; the wildcard mask requires that the first and second octet decimal numbers match and that the last two octets can be any number. Answer B is incorrect; the second octet must match as required by the wildcard mask. **Answer C is correct; the wildcard mask requires that the first and second octet decimal numbers match and that the last two octets can be any number.** Answer D is incorrect; the first octet of the address does not match the first octet of the address in the access list, as required by the wildcard mask.

3. Wildcard mask bits of 1 are used to specify that a packet's address must match that particular bit in the access list address.

A. True

B. False

Answer A is incorrect; a 1 bit in the wildcard mask means that the bit in the packet address should be ignored. **Answer B is correct; it is 0 bits in a wildcard mask that require the packet address bit to be compared to the address bit in the access list for filtering to take place.**

4. Which command is valid to associate a standard IP access list to an interface at the interface configuration prompt, where packets would be filtered entering the interface?

A. `ip access-group 1 out`

B. `ip access-group 100 in`

C. `ip access-group 1 in`

D. `ipx access-group 1 in`

Answer A is incorrect; the access list is grouped to the interface to filter outgoing packets. Answer B is incorrect; the access list number 100 is for extended IP access lists, not standard lists. **Answer C is correct; this command groups a standard access list number (1) to the interface so that incoming packets are filtered.** Answer D is incorrect; this command is for an IPX access list grouping with an interface, and the access list number (1) is not appropriate for the command syntax.

5. Which of these access list statements filters packets originating from an FTP client?

A. `access-list 100 deny tcp 129.5.0.0 0.0.255.255 host`
`10.1.1.1 eq 23`

B. `access-list 100 deny udp 129.5.0.0 0.0.255.255 host`
    `10.1.1.1 eq 21`

C. `access-list 100 deny tcp 129.5.0.0 0.0.255.255 host`
    `10.1.1.1 eq 21`

D. `access-list 100 deny tcp 129.5.0.0 0.0.255.255 host`
    `10.1.1.1 lt 21`

Answer A is incorrect; this access list statement denies packets using socket 23, which is Telnet. Answer B is incorrect; the transport protocol for FTP (port 21) is TCP, not UDP. **Answer C is correct; this access list command uses the correct transport protocol and provides the port number for FTP (21).** Answer D is incorrect; the `lt` statement before the port number designation (21) means less than 21; therefore, protocols with well-known port numbers of less than 21 will be filtered.

6. Which commands provide a listing of IP interfaces and access lists grouped to them (select all that apply)?

   A. `show ip interface`
   B. `show access-lists`
   C. `show ip access-lists`
   D. `show running-config`

Answer A is correct; this command provides a list of IP-enabled interfaces and any access lists associated with them. Answer B is incorrect; this command lists only access lists on the router, not the interfaces with which they are associated. Answer C is incorrect; the command lists only IP access lists on the router, not the interfaces with which they are associated. **Answer D is correct; this command shows access lists and their grouping to router interfaces.**

7. Standard IPX access lists are designated by the range of numbers:

   A. 1–99
   B. 1000–1099
   C. 100–199
   D. 800–899

Answer A is incorrect; this is the range for standard IP access lists. Answer B is incorrect; this is the range for specifying SAP filters. Answer C is incorrect; this is the range for extended IP access lists. **Answer D is correct; this is the range used to specify a standard IPX access list.**

8. SAP filters that filter output are associated with an interface with the command:

A. `ip access-group [access list #] out`

B. `ipx output-sap-filter [access-list number]`

C. `ipx access-group [access list #] out`

D. `ipx input-sap-filter [access-list number]`

Answer A is incorrect; this is the command used to associate an IP access list to an interface to filter outgoing packets. **Answer B is correct; this command associates a SAP filter with an interface and filters outgoing information from the SAP table.** Answer C is incorrect; this command is used to group IPX access lists to a particular interface. Answer D is incorrect; this command is used to link a SAP filter to an interface where input information is filtered from the SAP table.

9. To view the number of collisions experienced on an Ethernet 0 interface in a router, you would use the command

A. `show interface tokenring 0`

B. `ping`

C. `trace`

D. `show interface ethernet 0`

Answer A is incorrect; this command is used to view information related to a Token-Ring interface. Answer B is incorrect; `ping` can show only whether two devices are connected over the network; it does not supply any statistics. Answer C is incorrect; `trace` provides the route between two devices, not the number of collisions. **Answer D is correct; this command lists all the statistics related to the Ethernet 0 interface, including the number of collisions.**

10. One of your remote networks is experiencing a real lag time in receiving new data. You can ping remote hosts on the remote network, but you have a sneaking suspicion that a router is down and packets are being routed by a fairly circuitous route to the remote network. You can test this theory with which command?

A. `show interface`

B. `extended ping`

C. `trace`

D. `show running configuration`

233

Answer A is incorrect; although, if you are using IGRP as your routing protocol, you might see the reliability of this interface go down in relation to earlier reliability statistics. Answer B is incorrect; although it can be used with other protocols (other than IP) such as IPX, extended ping still provides only a yes or no answer on node connectivity. **Answer C is correct; trace shows the new route being used to route the packets from the local router to the remote network.** Answer D is incorrect; this command provides only a list of configuration settings you have set up on the router; it provides no diagnostic information whatsoever.

Cheat Sheet

Access lists take the form of `permit` or `deny` statements, which are then associated with a particular router interface that is enabled for the networking protocol stack being filtered.

IP standard and extended access lists use a wildcard mask with source or destination IP addresses (destination addresses are used only in the case of extended IP access lists). The wildcard mask is a 32-bit mask that uses a 0 when a bit in a packet's address should be compared to a bit in the access list statement. It uses a 1 when bits should not be compared.

Table 11.3 summarizes access list types and their various attributes.

Table 11.3 Access List Summary

Access List Type	Numerical Range	Filter By	Command Syntax
Standard IP	1–99	Source IP address	`access-list 1-99 permit/deny [source address] [wildcard mask]`
Extended IP	100–199	Source IP address; destination address; protocol; port number	`access-list 100-199 permit/deny [protocol] [source] [destination] [port]`
Standard IPX	800–899	Source address; destination address	`access-list 800-899 permit/deny [source] [destination]`
Extended IPX	900–999	Source address; destination address; IPX protocol; IPX socket	`access-list 900-999 permit/deny [source] [socket] [destination] [socket]`

Continued

Table 11.3 continued

Access List Type	Numerical Range	Filter By	Command Syntax
SAP Filters	1000–1099	Source address; service type	`access-list 1000-1099 permit/deny [source] [service type]`

IP access lists (both standard and extended) are grouped to an interface using the command

```
ip access-group [list number] [in or out]
```

Common port numbers used in extended IP access lists:

Protocol	Port Number
HTTP	80
FTP	21
TFTP	69
SMTP	25
SNMP	161
DNS	53
Telnet	23

SAP filters are associated with an interface so that they filter either input or output of SAP information related to that interface. The commands for filtering input and output, respectively, are as follows:

```
ipx input-sap-filter [access-list number]
```

```
ipx output-sap-filter [access-list number]
```

The show access-lists command provides a listing of all access lists configured on the router (including IPX access lists).

The show ip access-lists command provides a list of IP access lists only.

The show ip interface command provides a listing of IP-enabled interfaces on the router and any access lists that have been grouped to specific interfaces.

The show running-config command provides a listing of the running configuration, including access lists grouped to various router interfaces.

The show ipx access-lists command provides a list of IPX access lists on the routers.

The show ipx interface command provides a listing of IPX interfaces and associated access lists.

Useful troubleshooting commands:

- show interface ethernet [interface #]—Provides statistics and configuration settings related to an Ethernet interface on the router.
- show interface tokenring [interface #]—Provides statistics and configuration settings related to a Token-Ring interface on a router.
- show interface serial [interface #]—Provides statistics and configuration settings related to a serial interface on a router.
- ping—Used to verify the connection between two devices on the network.
- trace—Provides the routing sequence for packets moving from a source device to a destination device.

LAN Design and Segmentation

Cisco has divided its CCNA exam objectives into nine categories. Category 7 is "LAN Design" and covers objectives related to Ethernet and Token-Ring local area network design. Category 1 covers bridging/switching, which concentrates on layer two switches and bridges. Category 9 is "Cisco Basics, IOS, and Network Basics" and also includes subject matter related to switching and the Cisco switch IOS. This chapter covers all the objectives in Category 7, Category 1 (precluding PPP, which is discussed in Chapter 10, "WAN Protocols—Configuring PPP and ISDN"), and Category 9 related to LAN design and switches and bridges (see the following objectives list).

- Ethernet
- Fast Ethernet
- Gigabit Ethernet
- Token-Ring
- VLANs
- Spanning-Tree protocol
- Switching modes/methods
- IOS CLI Switch

30

Ethernet

Ethernet is the most commonly deployed network architecture in the world (80% of all network implementations are Ethernet). The specifications for running Ethernet have been defined by the Institute of Electrical and Electronic Engineers (IEEE), and its designation is IEEE 802.3. Ethernet runs at the OSI model's Data Link layer.

Ethernet provides access to the network using carrier sense multiple access with collision detection (CSMA/CD). This strategy of network access basically means that the nodes on the network listen (sense) to the network and wait until the line is clear. The computer then sends its packets out onto the line. If more than one computer is transmitting, collisions result. Sensing the collisions, the computer then stops transmitting and waits until the line is free. One of the computers then transmits, gaining control of the line and completing the transmission of packets.

Because Ethernet is a passive—wait and listen—architecture, collisions are common on the network, and computers must contend for transmission time. Therefore, large Ethernet networks must be segmented using internetworking devices such as bridges, switches, and routers (which are discussed later in the chapter). Ethernet networks typically are found in a star bus configuration (hubs daisy-chained together into a bus with the computers attached to the hubs in a star formation). One of the common implementations of Ethernet runs on twisted-pair wire at 10Mbps and is called 10BASE-T (typically Category 5 twisted-pair is used). Other 10Mbps implementations of Ethernet are described in Table 12.1.

Table 12.1 Ethernet Implementations

Ethernet Designation	Cable Type	Maximum Cable Length	Connector Types
10BASE-T	CAT 5 UTP	100 meters	RJ-45 male and female connection on cables and hubs, respectively
10BASE-2	Thinnet	185 meters	T connectors, barrel connectors, terminators
10BASE-5	Thicknet	500 meters	Vampire taps, transceiver drop cables, terminators
10BASE-FL	Fiber-optic	2 kilometers	Repeaters, terminators

Because the way Ethernet works inherently leads to bandwidth problems, strategies have been developed to maximize the bandwidth available to users. Segmentation has already been mentioned and is discussed in more detail later in the chapter. Faster implementations of Ethernet, fast Ethernet (100Mb), and gigabit Ethernet (1000Mb), have also been developed and are discussed in the two sections that follow.

Another way to maximize the available bandwidth on an Ethernet networks is to implement *full-duplex* Ethernet. *Half-duplex* Ethernet (the norm since 1984) enables a computer to send information and receive information but not concurrently. This is because the computer must listen for any collisions related to the sending of data frames. Therefore, it cannot use the second wire to receive data during the act of sending. This means when a computer is sending data, it must complete its transmission before it can accept data from another node on the network.

Full-duplex Ethernet requires full-duplex network cards and provides a point-to-point connection between the computer transmitting and the computer receiving. The full-duplex circuitry enables a computer to transmit and receive data at the same time (switches providing full-duplex ports would be part of the network's infrastructure). This maximizes the use of the bandwidth available on the network.

Fast Ethernet

Fast Ethernet is so named because of its "faster" throughput speed (when compared to the 10Mbps flavor of Ethernet). Fast Ethernet provides a bandwidth of 100Mbps. This faster throughput is due to the fact that the time it takes to transmit a bit of information over the Ethernet channel has been reduced by a factor of 10. So, Fast Ethernet is capable of running 10 times faster than 10Mbps Ethernet, providing the 100Mbps throughput. The frame format and the amount of data in each frame remains consistent in this higher-speed version of Ethernet (again when using 10Mbps Ethernet as the standard).

Implementations of Fast Ethernet were initially used as network backbones but have now been integrated into the LAN infrastructure itself, particularly because of users' need for more bandwidth. Fast Ethernet backbones are rapidly being replaced by FDDI backbones and ATM switching environments (ATM is discussed in Chapter 9, "WAN Protocols—HDLC Frame Relay and ATM").

While 100BASE-T is the IEEE standard for Fast Ethernet and compliant with the 802.3 Ethernet standards, another flavor of 100Mbps networking is available—100VG-AnyLAN. This high-speed data communication standard can be used on both Ethernet and Token-Ring networks (Token-Ring is discussed later in this chapter). Remembering the "AnyLAN" portion of this networking standards name will help you remember that it can be implemented on both Ethernet and Token-Ring. Remember also that 100VG-AnyLAN is not compliant with the IEEE 802.3 standards for Fast Ethernet.

The 802.3 Fast Ethernet standard comes in several flavors, as follows:

- **100BASE-TX**—Uses Category 5 UTP cabling. This implementation can also use 100-ohm shielded twisted-pair. Maximum cable distance without a repeater is 100 meters.

- **100BASE-T4**—Fast Ethernet over Category 3–5 cabling using standard RJ45 connectors. Maximum cable length is the standard twisted-pair reach of 100 meters.

- **100BASE-FX**—Fast Ethernet over fiber-optic cable. The maximum cable distance with no signal enhancement is 412 meters.

The obvious benefit of Fast Ethernet is the greater bandwidth available (especially in switched environments in which users are provided with dedicated bandwidth). Another plus of Fast Ethernet is that the existing cabling (Category 3 or better) can be used in the Fast Ethernet implementation. Internetworking equipment (such as switches, routers, and hubs) will have to be upgraded for Fast Ethernet compatibility and computers will require that network interface cards be upgraded to Fast Ethernet NICs.

Gigabit Ethernet

Gigabit Ethernet also embraces the 802.3 standards and therefore uses the CSMA/CD method of accessing the network medium. In addition, Gigabit Ethernet uses the same frame format and frame size as the other Ethernet implementations we've discussed. Because Gigabit Ethernet can also operate in full-duplex mode, it is currently deployed as a backbone between full-duplex switches. However, with the endless hunger for bandwidth at the desktop, it's only a matter of time until Gigabit Ethernet will be deployed at the workstation level.

Gigabit Ethernet (1000Mbps) currently runs over fiber-optic cable, but implementations over Category 5 unshielded twisted-pair (UTP) are becoming a reality. For the exam, know that Gigabit Ethernet is currently available over fiber and is often used to connect high-speed switches and specialized servers.

As far as a checklist of things to know about Gigabit Ethernet for the exam, see the list that follows:

- It uses the IEEE 802.3 Ethernet Frame Format.
- It uses CSMA/CD as the network access strategy (the same for all the IEEE-compliant Ethernets).
- It supports half-duplex and full-duplex at 1000Mbps.
- It is backward-compatible with earlier versions of Ethernet.
- Many specialized applications and network-monitoring devices currently deployed on Ethernet networks can be taken advantage of in the Gigabit environment.

Remember that Cisco has a vested interest in Gigabit technology and Gigabit-enabled switching products. Gigabit Ethernet also fits nicely into Cisco's implementations of ATM over ATM switches (ATM is discussed in

Chapter 9). Questions concerning the upgrading of networks to higher speeds will almost certainly mention Fast Ethernet, Gigabit Ethernet, and ATM switches as strategies for supplying greater bandwidth to the desktop user.

33

Token-Ring

IBM Token-Ring is characterized as a fast and reliable network that uses token passing as its media access strategy. Token-Ring networks are wired in a star configuration with a multi-station access unit (MAU) providing the central connection for the nodes on the LAN. The actual ring on which the token is circulated (the token moves in one direction as characterized by the ring topology) is a logical ring inside the MAU.

The token is passed around the ring until a computer wanting to send information out onto the network takes possession of the token. A computer that passes the token to the next computer on the logical ring is called the *nearest active upstream neighbor (NAUN)*. The computer being passed the token is the *nearest active downstream neighbor (NADN)*.

After a computer takes possession of the token and transmits data, it then passes a new token to its NADN, and the token makes its way around the ring until a node on the network takes possession to transmit.

The specifications for running IBM Token-Ring architecture have been defined by the IEEE, and its designation is IEEE 802.5. Token-Ring runs at the OSI model's Data Link layer.

Token-Ring is characterized by no collisions and equal access to the network media by all the nodes on the network. It is slower than some implementations of Ethernet (Token-Ring can run at 4Mbps and 16Mbps), but the network degrades more gracefully during times of high traffic (although a Gigabit implementation of Token-Ring is now available).

Token-Ring also provides some fault tolerance to the network by having an error detection strategy called beaconing. When the computers on the network are first brought online, the first computer powered on is designated as the Active Monitor. The Active Monitor sends out a data packet every seven seconds that travels around the ring to help determine whether any of the nodes on the network are finished. For example, if a particular computer does not receive the packet from its NAUN, it creates a packet containing its address and the NAUN's address and sends the packet onto the network. This packet provides information that the Token-Ring can actually use to automatically reconfigure the ring and maintain network traffic.

34

Network Segmentation and VLANs

VLANs (virtual local area networks) are used to group computers and other network devices into broadcast domains, regardless of the computers' or devices' physical locations. This is accomplished by grouping particular ports on a LAN switch in a VLAN.

Because each VLAN is a separate broadcast domain, broadcast and multicast messages within the VLAN are isolated from the rest of the network. Also, segmenting a large network into VLANs using a switch or switches reduces the number of devices on a particular segment, which increases the available bandwidth.

To fully understand the use and configuration of VLANs (I mean "fully understand" in the context of what you need to know for the CCNA exam), you must understand some basics related to network segmentation. Because network congestion is one of the network administrator's greatest enemies, particularly on Ethernet networks, hardware solutions have been developed to preserve network bandwidth. As network traffic increases on an Ethernet network, so do collisions, which robs the network of valuable bandwidth. Three devices—bridges, switches, and routers—can be used to segment a network (because routers are discussed in detail in other chapters in this book, the next two sections discuss bridges and switches, respectively).

Bridges

Bridges are Data Link layer devices (Layer 2) that operate at the MAC sublayer, using the MAC addresses on frames to determine whether they should be forwarded from one segment to another. Transparent bridges are employed on Ethernet networks, whereas Source-Routing bridges are employed on Token-Ring networks. Bridges forward packets (or drop packets that are part of local segment traffic) on the network based on a bridging table.

The bridge builds the table by sampling the packets received on its various ports until it has a complete list of the MAC addresses for each segment on the network. This forwarding table is then used to determine whether data traffic is local to a particular segment (for example, data being sent from one computer to another on the same segment). If the traffic is local, the bridge does not forward the traffic and drops the frames because it assumes they've reached their destination.

Bridges do, however, forward broadcast packets from the various nodes on the network to all the segments (such as NetBIOS and other broadcasts). Also, in cases where the bridge is unable to resolve a MAC address to a particular segment on the network, it forwards the packets to all the connected segments. This can lead to broadcast storms on the network.

Bridges actually physically segment the LAN network into several segments (see the following figure). Rather than actually breaking a network into subnetworks—also called *subnets*—like a router does and managing traffic by switching data on particular routes, bridges filter traffic to conserve bandwidth. The bridging table manages the filtering.

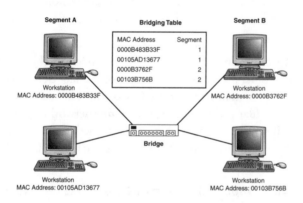

One problem related to bridges is *latency*. Latency is the time it takes for a frame to travel from the source to the destination. If a great deal of traffic is present on the destination segment, the bridge must wait to forward the frame to the destination host. One way to overcome latency and also provide fault tolerance to the networked bridge is the use of multiple physical paths between the nodes on the network. Path redundancy using multiple physical paths and issues related to them is discussed in the section "The Spanning-Tree Protocol," later in this chapter.

Switches

Switches are similar to bridges in that they forward packets to a particular segment using MAC hardware addressing; however, switches provide greater port density and some other enhancements that we will discuss in this section. These enhancements make switches superior to the standard bridges. The fact that switches can have a high number of ports means that each user's workstation can be assigned a unique port, which provides the user with dedicated bandwidth. This enables devices on the LAN to take full advantage of the network medium; for example, users on a 10MB Ethernet network can realize a bandwidth of 10Mb. In addition, Gigabit Ethernet users can be assigned up to 1,000Mb of bandwidth.

Switch hardware also can take advantage of full-duplex access to the network media. This enables the sending and receiving of data simultaneously on the network. This also provides network access on an Ethernet network that would essentially be collision free. A node on a Fast Ethernet network, which runs at 100Mbps, would actually realize a net total of 200Mbps throughput because of the fact that sending and receiving can take place simultaneously on the full-duplex media.

Because this is Cisco's exam, some discussion of Cisco switching products is appropriate here. You should at least be aware of the fact that three major families of switches are manufactured by Cisco and that each family is designed for a particular purpose in regard to internetworking solutions for networks of varying scale. All the switches mentioned are modular in design and can be outfitted with various LAN modules, such as 100BASE-T, ATM, or FDDI:

- **Cisco Catalyst 1900 and 2820 switches**—These two switch families are considered entry-level switches for companies moving from the traditional LAN infrastructure to switched LANs (in terms of cost and features). Each of these switch types provides several models with various port densities (number of ports). Most switches in these two families can also run different versions of the switch IOS: standard and enterprise. The enterprise version of the switch IOS provides the greatest flexibility and the capability to implement multiple VLANs on the network. The IOS command set for these switches is menu-based, making them relatively easy to configure.

- **Cisco Catalyst 2900 Series switches**—This family of switches is relatively new when compared to the other families of Cisco switches. They provide some additional flexibility and capability when compared to the 1900 and 2820 switches. The 2900 series uses the same IOS CLI (command-line interface) as the 5000 series and provides several models. It is considered a step up from the 1900 and 2820s.

- **Cisco Catalyst 5000 Series switches**—The Catalyst 5000 series are enterprise-level switches that provide high performance and several models, depending on the size of the LAN and the intended implementation. The 5000 series is considered the most flexible of the switch families and has the capability to contend with high levels of network traffic, such as the level of traffic experienced by data centers. Although your knowledge of switches for the CCNA exam should revolve around layer 2 switching, the Catalyst 5000 switches do include some layer 3 functionality, which we typically consider the realm of routers. The 5000 series uses a command-line interface and command set that are similar to the IOS found on Cisco routers (we look at the switch CLI at the end of this chapter).

Switches basically have three functions: address learning, forwarding/filtering, and loop avoidance. *Address learning* means that the switch builds a MAC address table (much like a bridge) that is used to locate specific devices connected to the switch. MAC addresses are matched to port numbers in the table.

Forwarding/filtering is the action the switch takes when it receives a frame that has a known destination address (known to the switch). The frame is forwarded to the appropriate port, conserving the bandwidth on all other ports. This is in essence filtering as well as forwarding.

Because it is likely that redundant routes (to destination nodes) have been configured for data within the switched network, the switch must deploy some sort of strategy for avoiding switching loops, in which data moves in a circular path and is incapable of being switched to the final destination node. Cisco switches use the Spanning-Tree Protocol to avoid loops. Spanning-Tree is discussed later in this chapter.

One negative aspect related to switches is that they do forward broadcast and multicast frames to all nodes on the network. As is the case with bridges, this forwarding of broadcast data can result in broadcast storms, which can quickly bring down an Ethernet network.

Before we leave the switch subject matter that you will be required to know for the CCNA exam, be advised that the exam leans toward an understanding of VLANs and switching modes. If you plan to choose subsets of information that will help you get the most points on the test, these two areas are a must. VLANs having already been defined, are tackled in the next section. Switching modes is covered under a separate objective later in this chapter.

VLANs

As I already stated at the outset of this particular objective section, a VLAN is a logical subnetwork configured internally on the switch, and it groups switch ports together regardless of the actual devices' physical locations. This divides a larger network into smaller collision domains. For example, you might have engineers housed on different floors of a building, but you can group them into the same VLAN by grouping the appropriate switch ports.

VLANs provide several benefits:

- Traffic is distributed across the VLANs, controlling overloading of a particular segment.

- The network becomes highly scalable because segmentation using VLANs can be applied on an as needed basis.

- The relocation of workers and the addition or movement of equipment is easily handled because the VLAN structure does not rely on physical location.

- VLAN segmentation enables the control of broadcast packets on the network.

Because switches operate at the Data Link layer of the OSI model and use MAC addresses to move packets, VLANs are not limited to a particular IP subnet. Therefore, if you physically move a workstation or a server, the device can remain on its associated VLAN. So, a major benefit of VLANs is reduced administration and reduced administrative costs.

Although you are not required to know the command set for creating VLANs and assigning ports to a VLAN for the CCNA exam, you should know some of the general aspects of configuring VLANs on switches that support them (this depends on the IOS being run on the switch).

One rule of VLAN configuration is that each port on the switch can belong to only one particular VLAN. However, because rules are meant to be broken, switches that support trunking—such as the Catalyst 5000 series—do enable ports to be configured as trunking ports, which in turn allows the port to belong to more than one VLAN. (The operating system of the switch supports the Inter Switch Link protocol [ISL], which provides the trunking capability.) Trunking is particularly useful when interconnecting switches because a port can support more than one VLAN. This trunking capability (found in the Enterprise version of the IOS on most Catalyst switches) is what enables the existence of VLANs across multiple switches.

Another method that is used to enable frames to be switched through multiple switch devices is *frame tagging*. Frame tagging places a unique user-defined ID in the header of the frame as the frame is forwarded onto the switched network (you might find the term switch fabric used to describe the complex topology of a switched network). This identifier is examined and used by switches to move the frame from port to port. When the frame exits the switch fabric, the frame tag is removed from the header of the frame and the frame is then forwarded to the destination device for the data.

35

The Spanning-Tree Protocol

Because bridged and switched networks can be configured to supply redundant data paths, some sort of mechanism is required to negate a data loop on the network. This is where the Spanning-Tree Protocol comes in. It is defined by the IEEE standard 802.1d. The Spanning-Tree Protocol was developed to prevent loops in networks that use bridges, switches, and routers and to provide redundant data paths through the network framework. The Spanning-Tree Protocol is used by internetworking devices to allow certain paths through the network and denies others. This creates a loop-free environment on the network.

For the CCNA exam, you must know the basics of how the Spanning-Tree Protocol works, particularly in a switched network environment. It calculates a loop-free network topology using frames called *configuration bridge protocol data units (BPDUs)*. BPDUs are sent by each network switch and received by each network switch. The BPDU frames also are processed by the switches (they don't forward the BPDUs) and are used to determine the loop-free route in the network.

This exchange of information between the switches using the BPDUs sets up some ports on a switch or other device as blocking ports and other ports as forwarding ports—basically opening and closing doors to create the loop-free topology. Even though the Spanning-Tree Protocol can calculate a loop-free route through the network (it is, after all, an algorithm that computes the best path), it does not guarantee that the network will be free of loops.

Switching Modes/Methods

Switches can actually process and transmit packets using various modes or methods. You should know the different switching methods and how they vary for the exam. One of the issues related to these methods is latency, or the time it takes to actually process the frame and move it on to its destination. You will see that one method reduces latency by minimally processing the frame, whereas the other method processes the entire frame before forwarding it. This might cause higher latency, but it does keep fragments and frames with errors off the network, which conserves bandwidth.

The switching modes are as follows:

- **Store-and-Forward**—This type of switching method is pretty self-explanatory. The switch copies the entire frame into its memory buffer and stores it until it processes the cyclical redundancy check (CRC), which is in the trailer of the frame, to determine whether the frame has an error. If the frame is error-free, it is forwarded. However, if the frame contains an error, it is dropped. Obviously, this switching method has a high latency, in that the buffer holds the frame while it is processed by the switch.

- **Cut-Through Switching**—As the name implies, this method of switching "cuts to the chase," reducing the latency time. Cut-through switches read the destination address of the frame (found in the header), check the switching table, and then immediately forward the frame to the appropriate port. Although this method certainly speeds the frame on its way, it does not stop fragments and frames with errors from being forwarded onto the network, which takes up bandwidth.

- **Fragment-Free**—This type of switching method is a compromise between store-and-forward and cut-through switching. The switch reads the first 64 bytes of the frame into the buffer before forwarding the frame. Because most errors occur in the first 64 bytes and runts are typically less than 64 bytes (*runts* is the term used by Cisco to describe fragments), this method of switching provides less latency than store-and-forward and more latency than cut-through switching. However, this method does reduce the number of damaged frames floating around on the network.

IOS CLI Switch

You will find that any questions on the exam related to IOS commands or the IOS CLI (command-line interface) center on the Cisco router operating system. However, you should also be aware of how the switch CLI (particularly for the 5000 series of switches) is similar to the router IOS and shares several commands.

I mentioned earlier that the Cisco 1900 and 2800 series of switches use a menu-driven IOS for switch configuration and monitoring. The 2900 series and 5000 series both give you the option of working from the command line (products such as CiscoWorks and the Web-based command set on the 2900 series actually negate the need for configuring the switches from the CLI). Let's look at some basic switch commands and again notice the similarity between these commands and commands used on the router CLI.

The switch IOS offers a basic user mode in which the switch's settings can be viewed (primarily with the show command). The switch also offers a privileged mode that is reached by using the enable command and providing the appropriate privileged mode password.

You will find that many of the router commands with which you are familiar are also available at the switch CLI. For example, the show command is commonly used on the router and can be accompanied by a variety of parameters that provide you with an in-depth look at configuration settings on the router. The switch IOS also embraces the show command. The following figure shows the show interface VLAN1 command, which provides a summary of the VLAN1 configuration on the switch.

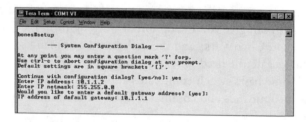

The switch CLI also offers a setup command that enables you to set the IP address and other parameters for a switch. This command is invoked at the privileged prompt by typing setup and then pressing Enter. Again, the setup command is also found as part of the router IOS. The following figure shows the results of the setup command on a switch.

As with the router IOS, a list of commands in a particular mode can be shown onscreen by typing a question mark (?) and pressing Enter. The following figure shows some of the commands available in privileged mode.

The switch also has a configuration mode that can be reached from the privileged prompt using the config command. To save configuration changes to the NVRAM on the router, use the write mem command. This command is actually the command that preceded the copy `run start` command in IOS 11.x for the routers. Cisco has gone to great lengths to keep its internetworking device operating systems as similar as possible.

TAKE THE TEST

This Practice Test provides you with questions related to eight of the objectives for the CCNA exam. This chapter covered material in three exam preparation categories. Category 7, "LAN Design," contains the objectives Ethernet, Fast Ethernet, Gigabit Ethernet, and Token-Ring. Category 1 contains the objectives Static VLANs, Spanning-Tree, and Switching Modes/Methods. Category 9, "Cisco Basics, IOS and Network Basics," contains the IOS CLI Switch objective. Because the CCNA exam is in a multiple-choice format, these questions are formatted as they would be on the actual exam.

1. The IEEE designation for Ethernet is

   A. 802.5

   B. 802.1d

   C. 802.3

   D. 802.10

Answer A is incorrect; 802.5 is the IEEE designation for Token-Ring. Answer B is incorrect; 802.1d is the designation for the Spanning-Tree Protocol used on switches and bridges. **Answer C is correct; 802.3 is the IEEE designation for the Ethernet standard.** Answer D is incorrect; 802.10 is the IEEE designation for Network Security standards.

2. Which of the following network architectures is not compliant with the IEEE 802.3 standard?

   A. 10BASE-FL

   B. 100BASE-TX

   C. 100VG-AnyLAN

   D. Gigabit Ethernet

Answer A is incorrect; this is the designation for 10Mbps Ethernet over fiber-optic cable, which does comply with the 802.3 standard. Answer B is incorrect; this is the designation for Fast Ethernet over UTP cable, which is compliant with the 802.3 Ethernet standard. **Answer C is correct; 100VG-AnyLAN is not compliant with the IEEE 802.3 standard for Fast Ethernet.** Answer D is incorrect; Gigabit Ethernet is complaint with the 802.3 standard.

3. Which of the following network architectures degrades the most gracefully under high network use?

   A. Ethernet

   B. Token-Ring

   C. Gigabit Ethernet

   D. Full-duplex Ethernet

Answer A is incorrect; as traffic builds on an Ethernet network, so does the number of collisions, which eventually can bring down the network. **Answer B is correct; Token-Ring provides more equal access to the network medium via token passing, which enables the network to degrade more gracefully under high use.** Answer C is incorrect; Gigabit Ethernet faces the same types of traffic and collision issues that 10Mbps Ethernet does. Answer D is kind of a ringer. Full-duplex will cut down on the possibility of collisions, so the answer is correct in certain respects. However, even a full-duplex Ethernet implementation can suffer collisions and the subsequent loss of bandwidth.

4. Two devices that operate at the Data Link Layer of the OSI model are

   A. Bridge

   B. Repeater

   C. Router

   D. Switch

Answer A is correct; bridges operate at the Data Link layer of the OSI model. Answer B is incorrect; repeaters operate at the Physical layer of the OSI model. Answer C is incorrect; routers operate at the Network layer of the OSI model. **Answer D is correct; switches operate at the Data Link layer of the OSI model.**

5. Switches have three basic functions:

   A. Routing

   B. Forwarding/filtering

   C. Address learning

   D. Loop avoidance

Answer A is incorrect; switches do not have Network layer functionality, which is used by routers to make routing decisions. **Answer B is correct; switches do forward and filter frames based on their destination MAC hardware addresses. Answer C is correct; switches do have the capability to build switching tables that contain port and MAC hardware addressing information. Answer D is correct; switches are designed to avoid loops using the Spanning-Tree Protocol.**

6. Which of the following are true concerning VLANs (select all that apply)?

   A. VLANs can consist of only computers on one subnet.

   B. The use of VLANs makes it easy to relocate workers and equipment to different physical locations.

   C. VLANs are logical subnetworks of grouped switch ports.

   D. Users on a particular VLAN must be in the same physical proximity on the network.

Answer A is incorrect; VLANs by definition are capable of grouping computers together from different locations and IP subnets. **Answer B is correct; the logical VLAN enables you to group users anywhere on the network and maintain the logical grouping even if a particular user is moved to a new physical location. Answer C is correct; a VLAN is a logical grouping of switch ports.** Answer D is incorrect; users can be anywhere on the physical network and still be grouped into a particular VLAN.

7. Which of the following technologies increases the available bandwidth on an Ethernet network (select all that apply)?

   A. Fast Ethernet

   B. VLANs

   C. Gigabit Ethernet

   D. Segmentation with a bridge

Answer A is correct; Fast Ethernet provides a throughput on the network 10 times greater than that of 10Mbps Ethernet. Answer B is correct; VLANs enable you to segment the network with switches and create separate broadcast domains within the larger network. Answer C is correct; Gigabit Ethernet supplies 1000Mbps throughput, greatly increasing the bandwidth available to users on the network. Answer D is correct; segmenting a network with a bridge can be used to keep local traffic on a particular segment rather than allowing the traffic to pervade the entire network.

8. Which of the following router IOS commands are also available at the Cisco switch CLI (select all that apply)?

   A. show

   B. setup

   C. config

   D. enable

Answer A is correct; the show command can be used to view switch settings in both the user and privileged modes. Answer B is correct; the setup command is used on the switch to enter the initial configuration dialog, as is done on a router. Answer C is correct; the config command is used on the switch (when in the privileged mode) to enter the configuration mode. Answer D is correct; the switch, just like a router, has a privileged mode that is entered using the enable command.

Cheat Sheet

Ethernet is defined by the IEEE 802.3 standard and comes in a number of different permutations and physical configurations.

Ethernet Speed	Implementations
10Mbps	10BASE-T
	10BASE-2
	10BASE-5
	10BASE-FL
100Mbps	100BASE-TX
	100BASE-T4
	100BASE-FX
1000Mbps	Gigabit Ethernet is currently available over fiber-optic cable.

On switched Ethernet networks, full-duplex Ethernet can be realized, which enables computers on the network to send and receive data simultaneously.

The 100VG-AnyLAN standard can be used both on Ethernet and Token-Ring networks but is not compliant with the IEEE 802.3 standard for Fast Ethernet.

Token-Ring networks (IEEE 802.5) use a token passing strategy for media access. The passing of the token enables equal access for nodes to the network medium.

VLANs are logical subnetworks created on switched networks in which ports are grouped together into a VLAN.

Bridges can be used to segment networks to preserve bandwidth. They forward or drop packets based on the MAC addresses of data frames. Broadcast and multicast traffic is not filtered by a bridge.

Switches provide greater port density and speed when compared to bridges. Because switches support VLANs, they provide additional administrative opportunities to conserve and control the bandwidth on a switched network.

Because bridged and switched networks are often configured to provide redundant data paths through the network framework, the Spanning-Tree

Protocol was developed to negate data loops on the network. Switches communicate with bridge protocol data unit frames to share information that results in the loop-free network topology.

Cisco switches embrace three switching methods:

- Store and forward switching means that the entire frame and CRC are processed before the frame is forwarded to its destination.
- Cut-through switching examines the destination MAC address on the frame and then immediately forwards it.
- In fragment-free switching, the switch stores and examines the first part of the frame and then forwards intact frames and drops runts or frames with errors.

The Cisco switch CLI is similar to the router CLI and embraces several of the same commands:

Command	Use
show	Used with any number of parameters to view port settings and other switch configuration information
setup	Used to enter the switch's initial configuration dialog from the privileged prompt
enable	Used to enter the privileged mode from the user mode
config	Used to enter the configuration mode from the privileged mode
?	Executed at any prompt to view a list of available commands

The Student Preparation Guide

The CCNA Exam and This Book

This book can serve a couple of different functions as you prepare to take Cisco's CCNA exam 640-507. First of all, because this book is designed as a summary and quick reference of all the information necessary to pass the exam, you might want to go through the book quickly before you begin to use other study aids or courses to get an overview of the material you will need to know for the exam. This book is also designed to serve as a refresher to help you recall the information you might have gleaned from courses, other books, or hands-on experience with Cisco hardware, such as routers. So, it will serve you well as a final resource that can be studied during the last week prior to actually taking the exam.

To help you ensure that you have covered all the ground necessary to pass the test, Table A.1 summarizes the Cisco Exam categories and the individual objectives and maps them to the chapters in which they appear. You can use the table as a checklist as you become comfortable with each subject area.

Table A.1 CCNA Exam Categories and Objectives

Category and Objective	Chapter
Bridging/Switching	
Static VLANs	Chapter 12
Spanning-Tree	Chapter 12
Switching Modes/Methods	Chapter 12
PPP	Chapter 10

Table A.1 continued

Category and Objective	Chapter
OSI Reference Model and Layered Communication	
Layer Definitions	Chapter 1
Encapsulation/De-encapsulation	Chapter 1
Layer Functions	Chapter 1
Connection-Oriented Models	Chapter 2
Connectionless Models	Chapter 2
Model Benefits	Chapter 1
Network Protocols	
TCP/IP	Chapter 6
Novell IPX	Chapter 7
Windowing	Chapter 2
IPX	Chapter 7
Routing	
IGRP	Chapter 8
ICMP	Chapter 6
WAN Protocols	
ISDN	Chapter 10
Frame Relay	Chapter 9
HDLC	Chapter 9
ATM	Chapter 9
Network Management	
Access Lists	Chapter 11
Telnet	Chapter 3
DNS	Chapter 6
LAN Design	
Ethernet	Chapter 12
Fast Ethernet	Chapter 12
Gigabit Ethernet	Chapter 12
Token-Ring	Chapter 12

Table A.1 continued

Category and Objective	Chapter
Physical Connectivity	
IEEE Standards	Chapter 2
ANSI Standards	Chapter 2
Cisco Basics, IOS, and Network Basics	
IOS CLI Router	Chapter 3
Troubleshooting	Chapter 11
Router Packet Switching Modes	Chapter 8
IOS CLI Switch	Chapter 12

Passing the Exam

In my role as a college professor, I have heard many "reasons" for students having scored poorly on tests. And during my research for writing this book, I spoke with a number of CCNA candidates, some who passed the exam and some who did not.

One common thread that popped up in these conversations is the amount of actual preparation time it took to pass the CCNA exam successfully. Candidates who passed the exam were surprised at the long hours they spent doing both "book work" and hands-on training (on a router) before they were ready to take the exam. Unsuccessful candidates often stated that they felt they hadn't spent enough time preparing.

The amount of preparation time, of course, will greatly depend on the amount of time you are actually getting on the routers or spending in an environment that helps you learn all the theory necessary to pass the exam. If you are a network support specialist or work in some other position in which you spend time actually configuring Cisco routers and switches, it will probably take you only a matter of weeks to get all the theory down to pass the exam.

However, if you are currently working outside the technical arena and hope to use your CCNA certification as a "boost" into a new field, you need to start from scratch in terms of both hands-on and theory. I have had students who, after a 10-week introductory course to Cisco routers, have spent an additional 2–4 weeks cramming for the exam and then have passed it successfully.

How much time it takes you to prepare for the exam really must be gauged by you; but here are some general study tips that will help:

- Set aside "quiet time" for studying CCNA resources (such as this book), and study in a place where you will not be interrupted during the time frame you've set aside.

- Try to work on a particular CCNA subject area until you know it inside and out before moving on to the next group of objectives (as shown in Table A.1).

- Memorizing facts is a good start, but you must understand the concepts to pass the exam. Use your study materials to gain a working knowledge of both the theoretical and real-world aspects of protocols, the OSI model, and routing and switching. Cisco's questions are designed to make you think, so you must know and understand the material contained in this book if you want to become a CCNA.

- Don't bother with the CCNA brain dumps you find on the Web. Memorizing the answers to questions that have been dumped on the Web by people who have taken the exam might help you get a few correct answers on the test, but it won't help you understand the concepts related to routing and switching that you really need to know to pass the exam and then actually work in the field. Besides, brain dumps violate the non-disclosure agreement you make with Cisco when you actually take the test (and it is not uncommon for a brain dump answer to be wrong, anyway).

- If you have some material that is not sinking in, try to study those particular facts, concepts, or commands just before you go to bed. There is some truth to the notion that you remember things you read or do just prior to "hitting the hay."

- Have fun with the material. If you are trying to become a CCNA, you obviously want to work in the internetworking field. Make your learning experience enjoyable. Try to reward yourself after you have become comfortable with certain subject areas. And take your time; this isn't a race.

Registering for the Exam

If you have reached the point where you can successfully answer all the exam questions provided at the end of the chapters in this book and have scored well (upper 80% or better) on the practice tests you've taken on the accompanying CD-ROM, you are ready to take the exam. Before you can take the exam, however, you must register.

Testing for Cisco certifications such as the CCNA are handled by Sylvan Prometric (which is now known simply as Prometric). The cost for the CCNA exam is $100. You can register for the 640-507 CCNA exam by calling Prometric at 800-204-EXAM.

You also can register online at the Prometric Web site:

```
http://www.prometric.com/
```

When you register, you must provide the following information:

- Your name (as you want it to appear on your certificate)
- Your Social Security number (or Prometric identification number)
- Contact phone numbers
- Mailing address (use the address to which you want your certificate mailed)
- Exam number and title (in this case, Cisco's CCNA Exam 640-507)
- Email address (as an additional contact avenue)
- Credit card number (Prometric's preferred method of payment is by credit card, although you can pay by check or Prometric voucher; see Prometric's Web site for more information)

After you have registered for the exam, you should spend some time during each day leading up to the exam reviewing this book. Don't stop studying just because you have registered for the exam.

Taking the Exam

You will take your exam on a computer using an online testing tool. The CCNA 640-507 exam consists of 65 questions, and you are given 75 minutes to take the exam. The minimum passing score for the exam is 822 (based on a perfect score of 1000). The exam is in a multiple-choice format, although some questions use drag and drop in situations where you are asked to match material from one column to information in another column. Some questions also provide exhibits you must view before answering the question.

The CCNA exam does not provide you with the option of going back after you have answered a particular question. So, do not leave questions blank and move on to the next question, figuring you can come back to a question later. You get one shot at the answer, so take your time and choose wisely.

A counter does provide you with the elapsed time, so try to keep an eye on this as you work on the exam (but don't be consumed by the ticking of the clock).

Here are some other tips to help your test-taking be a little less stressful:

- Wear comfortable clothing. You want to focus on the exam, not on a tight shirt collar or a pinching pair of shoes.

- Allow plenty of travel time. Plan to arrive at the testing center 20–30 minutes early; nothing is worse than rushing in at the last minute (well, missing your assigned testing time is even worse). Give yourself time to relax before you sit down to take the exam.

- If you've never been to the testing center before, make a trial run a few days before to make sure you know the route to the center.

- Carry with you at least two forms of identification, including one photo ID (such as a driver's license or company security ID). You will have to show ID before you can take the exam.

During the test, take your time and select the best answer to each question. Try to eliminate the obviously incorrect answers first to clear away the clutter and simplify your choices. Also, remember to answer all the questions; you aren't penalized for guessing, and you might snag a correct answer or two in situations where you just can't seem to decide on a correct answer.

After the Exam

After you complete the exam, the testing tool gives you immediate notification of your pass or fail status. The exam administrator will give you a printed Examination Score Report indicating your pass or fail status and your exam results. Hang on to these results.

Exam scores are forwarded to Cisco. Typically, candidates who pass the exam (people like you) receive their CCNA certificate and a handy wallet card from Cisco within a few weeks of taking the exam.

If you pass the exam, congratulations (I think you will do just fine)! If you don't pass the exam, sit down immediately after taking the test and try to assess which subject areas gave you the most problems. Although it's painful, it's best to do this while the exam is still fresh in your mind. Study the areas you are weak in and then take the test again (when you are ready).

And while passing the exam is certainly a reward, remember that learning itself can be quite rewarding as well. Good luck, I'm rooting for you.

Index

What's on the CD-ROM

1. Test Engine

Que's new test engine, included on this CD-ROM, provides a variety of features to enhance your learning. This test engine has more than 250 questions built into its database to create a "fresh" test each time you take it. With each answer provided, you will be given a short explanation of the answer. The test engine also has a built-in timer to simulate the official CCNA 2.0 Exam. Unlike the official test, the timer can be paused for flexibility in your home study environment. Please note that the test engine requires your screen resolution to be 800×600.

To install the test engine, please go to the /TestEngine directory.

2. Electronic Book

Included on this CD-ROM is *CCNA 2.0 640-507 Routing and Switching Cheat Sheet* in the Acrobat Portable Document Format (PDF) by Adobe. There are also two sample chapters from other Que books for your perusal.

To view the book and chapters, please go to the /PDF directory.

3. Acrobat Reader by Adobe

The free Adobe Acrobat Reader enables you to view, navigate, and print PDF files across all major computing platforms. Acrobat Reader is the free viewing companion to both Adobe Acrobat and Acrobat Capture software.

Adobe Acrobat Reader's install is in the /3rdParty directory.

CD-ROM Installation

Windows 98/95/NT Installation Instructions

1. Insert the CD-ROM disc into your CD-ROM drive.

2. From the Windows 98/95/NT desktop, double-click the My Computer icon.

3. Double-click the icon representing your CD-ROM drive.

4. Double-click the icon titled START.EXE to run the CD-ROM interface.

NOTE

If Windows 98/95/NT is installed on your computer and you have the AutoPlay feature enabled, the START.EXE program starts automatically whenever you insert the disc into your CD-ROM drive.

Read This Before Opening the Software

By opening this package, you are agreeing to be bound by the following agreement:

You may not copy or redistribute the entire CD-ROM as a whole. Copying and redistribution of individual software programs on the CD-ROM is governed by terms set by the licensors or individual copyright holders.

The installer and code from the author(s) are copyrighted by the publisher and the author(s).

This software is sold as-is, without warranty of any kind, either expressed or implied, including but not limited to the implied warranties of merchantability and fitness for a particular purpose. Neither the publisher nor its dealers or distributors assumes any liability for any alleged or actual damages arising from the use of this program. (Some states do not allow for the exclusion of implied warranties, so the exclusion may not apply to you.)

NOTE: This CD-ROM uses long and mixed-case filenames requiring the use of a protected-mode CD-ROM Driver.